# LEADING
## AND
# SELLING

Leading and Selling: The Ultimate Toolkit For Success
by Digvijay Mourya
Paperback Edition

First published in India in 2023 by

Inkfeathers Publishing
Vivek Vihar, New Delhi
www.inkfeathers.com

ISBN 978-81-960895-2-8

# LEADING AND SELLING

## The Ultimate Toolkit for Success

DIGVIJAY MOURYA

Inkfeathers Publishing
www.inkfeathers.com

# DEDICATION

This book is dedicated to all the leaders and sales professionals who have the courage and determination to pursue their dreams and achieve their goals. Your hard work, passion, and commitment to excellence are an inspiration to me.

I would also like to dedicate this book to my family, loved ones, my office colleagues, and my Directors Mr. Deepak Verma & Mr. Praveen Verma, who have supported me throughout my journey. Your unwavering love, encouragement, and understanding have been instrumental in my success, and I am grateful for your constant support and belief in me.

Finally, I dedicate this book to all the readers who have chosen to invest their time and energy in learning and growing. I hope that this book will provide you with the knowledge, skills, and inspiration you need to succeed in leadership and sales and that it will help you achieve your own version of success.

Thank you for joining me on this journey. I wish you all the best in your pursuit of excellence.

# PREFACE

Welcome to "Leading and Selling: The Ultimate Toolkit for Success". In today's dynamic and competitive world, leadership and sales skills are essential for success in any field. Whether you are an entrepreneur, a business professional, or a student, mastering these skills will help you achieve your goals and maximize your potential.

This book is designed to provide you with a comprehensive toolkit for success in leadership and sales. It covers a wide range of topics, from the fundamentals of leadership and sales to advanced techniques and strategies. You will learn how to develop your leadership style, build effective teams, communicate with impact, and motivate others to achieve their goals. You will also learn how to prospect, qualify leads, negotiate deals, and close sales.

The book is organized into 2 parts. Part One focuses on leadership, covering topics such as leadership styles, team building, communication, and motivation. Part Two is dedicated to selling, and covers topics such as prospecting, qualifying leads, presenting solutions, negotiating, and closing deals.

Whether you are a seasoned professional or just starting out, this book will provide you with the knowledge, skills, and tools you need to succeed in leadership and sales.

We hope that you find this book informative and helpful and that it will inspire you to reach new heights in your personal and professional life.

Part One

# THE LEADER'S TOOLKIT

**Leadership** is the ability to guide and inspire a group of people toward a common goal or vision. A leader has the power to influence and motivate others to achieve their full potential, and to work together to accomplish a shared objective. Leadership involves taking responsibility for the success of a team or organization and making decisions that will help them achieve their goals. Effective leadership requires a combination of skills, including communication, problem-solving, decision-making, and emotional intelligence. A good leader must be able to understand and connect with their team, build trust, and respect, and create an environment that promotes growth and development. Ultimately, leadership is about creating a positive impact on the people and the world around you.

Leadership is important for several reasons:

1. **Achieving goals:** Leaders are responsible for setting goals and guiding their team towards achieving them. Without leadership, teams can lack direction, focus, and may struggle to achieve their objectives.
2. **Inspiring and motivating others:** A good leader has the ability to inspire and motivate their team members, encouraging them to work towards a common goal. Motivated employees tend to be more productive and engaged, resulting in a more successful organization.
3. **Building trust:** Leaders who are transparent, honest, and consistent in their actions build trust and respect within their

team. This trust can lead to more effective communication, better problem-solving, and increased collaboration.

4. **Managing change:** In today's rapidly changing business environment, leaders must be able to adapt and lead their teams through change. Effective leadership can help to manage resistance to change and create a positive culture that embraces innovation and continuous improvement.
5. **Developing future leaders:** Strong leaders are committed to developing the skills and abilities of their team members. By mentoring and coaching others, they can help to develop the next generation of leaders within the organization.

Overall, leadership is important because it helps organizations to achieve their goals and create a positive impact on their team members and the world around them.

There are several different **styles of leadership**, each with its own strengths and weaknesses. Here are some of the most common leadership styles:

1. **Autocratic leadership:** In this style, the leader makes all the decisions and closely controls the work of their team. This style can be effective in situations where quick decisions need to be made but can also create a lack of trust and respect among team members.
2. **Democratic leadership:** This style involves the leader involving their team in decision-making and seeking their input on important issues. This style can create a sense of ownership and engagement among team members but can also lead to slower decision-making and a lack of focus.
3. **Transformational leadership:** Transformational leaders inspire and motivate their team members to achieve their full potential. They focus on developing their team's skills and abilities and empowering them to make decisions and take ownership of their work.
4. **Servant leadership:** This style emphasizes the leader's responsibility to serve their team members, rather than the other way around. Servant leaders focus on meeting the needs of their team members and helping them to achieve their goals.
5. **Transactional leadership:** In this style, the leader rewards team members for achieving their goals and punishes them for failing to meet expectations. This style can be effective

in achieving short-term results but can also create a lack of creativity and innovation among team members.

6. **Laissez-faire leadership:** This style involves the leader providing minimal direction or guidance, and instead allowing their team members to make decisions and take ownership of their work. This style can be effective in situations where team members are highly skilled and motivated but can also lead to a lack of direction and accountability.

Overall, each leadership style has its own strengths and weaknesses, and the most effective leaders are often able to adapt their style to meet the needs of their team and the situation at hand.

**Self-awareness** is an essential component of effective leadership. It involves understanding your own strengths and weaknesses, recognizing your emotions and how they impact your behavior, and being able to accurately assess your own performance and the impact you have on others.

Here are some of the ways that self-awareness can benefit a leader:

1. **Improved decision-making:** Leaders who are self-aware are better able to make decisions that are aligned with their values and goals. They are also able to recognize their own biases and limitations, which can help them make more objective decisions.
2. **Better communication:** Self-aware leaders are able to communicate more effectively with their team members. They are able to listen actively, provide constructive feedback, and adjust their communication style to meet the needs of different team members.
3. **Increased emotional intelligence:** Leaders who are self-aware are better able to manage their own emotions and recognize the emotions of others. This can help them to build stronger relationships with their team members and create a more positive work environment.
4. **Improved performance:** Self-aware leaders are better able to identify areas where they need to improve and seek out opportunities for growth and development. They are also able to recognize their own successes and celebrate their

accomplishments, which can help to boost their confidence and motivation.

5. **Increased resilience:** Self-aware leaders are better able to cope with stress and setbacks. They are able to recognize when they are feeling overwhelmed and take steps to manage their stress levels, which can help them to maintain their focus and performance over the long term.

Overall, self-awareness is a key component of effective leadership. Leaders who are self-aware are better able to understand themselves and others, make better decisions, communicate more effectively, and achieve their goals.

**Developing self-awareness** can be a lifelong process, but there are several techniques that can help you become more self-aware. Here are some techniques:

1. **Mindfulness meditation:** Mindfulness meditation is a technique that involves focusing your attention on the present moment and observing your thoughts and feelings without judgment. Regular practice of mindfulness meditation can help you become more aware of your thoughts, emotions, and bodily sensations.
2. **Journaling:** Writing down your thoughts, feelings, and experiences in a journal can help you gain insight into your patterns of behavior and thought. Regular journaling can help you identify your strengths and weaknesses and become more aware of your emotions and how they affect your behavior.
3. **Seek feedback from others:** Asking for feedback from trusted friends, family, or colleagues can help you gain a different perspective on your behavior and identify blind spots that you may not be aware of.
4. **Reflection:** Taking time to reflect on your experiences and actions can help you gain insight into your behavior and thought patterns. Regular reflection can help you identify areas for personal growth and development.
5. **Self-reflection exercises:** There are several self-reflection exercises that can help you become more self-aware, such as creating a personal SWOT (Strengths, Weaknesses,

Opportunities, and Threats) analysis, creating a timeline of significant events in your life, or creating a gratitude journal.

By practicing these techniques, you can increase your self-awareness and develop a better understanding of yourself, your emotions, and your behavior.

**Self-awareness has numerous benefits**, both personally and professionally. Here are some of the key benefits:

1. **Improved emotional intelligence:** Self-awareness is a key component of emotional intelligence, which is the ability to understand and manage your own emotions as well as those of others. By developing self-awareness, you can become more in tune with your emotions and better manage them, leading to improved relationships with others.
2. **Improved decision-making:** When you are self-aware, you are better able to identify your values, goals, and priorities, which can help you make better decisions that align with what is most important to you.
3. **Improved communication:** Self-awareness can help you communicate more effectively with others because you are better able to understand your own thoughts and emotions and express them clearly and empathetically.
4. **Increased self-confidence:** When you are self-aware, you have a better understanding of your strengths and weaknesses, which can increase your self-confidence and help you pursue your goals with greater conviction.
5. **Better stress management:** Self-awareness can help you identify the triggers that cause stress and develop strategies to manage it more effectively.
6. **Improved personal relationships:** By developing self-awareness, you can improve your relationships with others by being more empathetic, understanding, and communicative.

Overall, self-awareness is a valuable tool that can help you navigate life's challenges with greater ease and achieve your goals with greater clarity and purpose.

**Communication skills** are essential for effective leadership. Here are some reasons why:

1. **Establishing a vision:** Effective communication skills are necessary to articulate a clear and compelling vision to your team. As a leader, you need to be able to communicate the "why" behind your team's work and inspire them to work towards a common goal.
2. **Building relationships:** Good communication skills are essential for building strong relationships with your team members, stakeholders, and customers. By being a good listener and communicator, you can build trust and rapport with others, which can help you achieve your goals.
3. **Providing feedback:** As a leader, you need to be able to provide constructive feedback to your team members. Effective communication skills are necessary to deliver feedback in a way that is clear, specific, and actionable.
4. **Resolving conflicts:** Conflicts are inevitable in any team or organization. Effective communication skills are necessary to resolve conflicts in a positive and constructive way and to ensure that all parties feel heard and valued.
5. **Inspiring action:** As a leader, you need to be able to inspire action and motivate your team to achieve their goals. Effective communication skills are necessary to articulate a clear plan of action and to communicate progress toward achieving goals.
6. **Managing change:** Effective communication skills are

necessary to manage change and to ensure that your team members are aligned with the changes you are making. By communicating the rationale behind the change and the expected outcomes, you can help your team navigate change more effectively.

In summary, effective communication skills are essential for leadership success. By mastering communication skills, you can inspire your team, build strong relationships, and achieve your goals with greater ease.

**Improving communication skills** takes practice and effort, but there are several techniques that can help.

Here are some techniques for improving communication skills:

1. **Active listening:** Active listening is the practice of fully concentrating on what the other person is saying, without distraction or interruption. To be an active listener, you should pay attention to the speaker's body language, tone of voice, and choice of words.
2. **Nonverbal communication:** Nonverbal communication includes body language, facial expressions, and tone of voice. By being aware of your own nonverbal cues, you can better understand how others perceive you and adjust your communication style accordingly.
3. **Clarity and conciseness:** When communicating, it's important to be clear and concise. Use simple language and avoid jargon or technical terms that may be unfamiliar to the listener.
4. **Empathy:** Empathy is the ability to understand and share the feelings of others. By being empathetic, you can better understand the perspectives and needs of others, which can help you communicate more effectively.
5. **Feedback:** Asking for feedback from others can help you identify areas for improvement in your communication skills. Be open to constructive feedback and use it to make changes to your communication style.

6. **Practice:** Effective communication skills take practice. Take opportunities to practice your communication skills, such as in meetings, presentations, or everyday conversations.
7. **Cultural awareness:** Be aware of cultural differences in communication styles, such as differences in body language, tone of voice, and use of language. Be respectful of cultural differences and adjust your communication style accordingly.

By practicing these techniques, you can improve your communication skills and become a more effective communicator in both personal and professional settings.

**Communication pitfalls are common mistakes** that people make when communicating, which can lead to misunderstandings, misinterpretations, and conflicts.

Here are some common communication pitfalls to avoid:

1. **Making assumptions:** Making assumptions can lead to misunderstandings and misinterpretations. Instead of assuming, ask questions and seek clarification.
2. **Not actively listening:** Not actively listening can lead to misunderstandings and can make the other person feel ignored or unimportant. To be an effective communicator, practice active listening.
3. **Using vague or unclear language:** Using vague or unclear language can lead to confusion and misinterpretation. Use clear language and be specific.
4. **Being defensive:** Being defensive can lead to conflicts and can make the other person feel attacked. Instead of being defensive, listen to the other person's perspective and be open to feedback.
5. **Not being empathetic:** Not being empathetic can make the other person feel misunderstood or unimportant. Practice empathy by putting yourself in the other person's shoes and understanding their perspective.
6. **Interrupting:** Interrupting can be seen as disrespectful and can prevent the other person from fully expressing their thoughts and feelings. Allow the other person to finish

speaking before responding.

7. **Not being aware of nonverbal cues:** Nonverbal cues, such as body language and tone of voice, can convey a lot of meaning. Be aware of your own nonverbal cues and the nonverbal cues of others.

By avoiding these common communication pitfalls, you can become a more effective communicator and build stronger relationships with others.

**Having a clear and compelling vision** is essential for individuals, organizations, and society as a whole. A vision is a forward-looking statement that sets out what an individual, organization, or society hopes to achieve in the future. It provides direction, purpose, and inspiration, and helps to align efforts towards a common goal.

Here are some reasons why having a vision is important:

1. **Provides Direction:** A clear vision helps to provide a sense of direction and purpose. It gives individuals, organizations, and society a clear idea of where they want to go and what they want to achieve.
2. **Inspires and Motivates:** A compelling vision inspires and motivates people to work towards a common goal. It creates a sense of excitement and enthusiasm and helps to build commitment and dedication.
3. **Facilitates Decision Making:** A vision provides a framework for decision-making. It helps individuals, organizations, and society to prioritize their efforts and allocate resources in a way that is aligned with their long-term goals.
4. **Fosters Innovation:** A vision encourages creativity and innovation. It inspires individuals and organizations to think outside the box and come up with new and innovative solutions to achieve their goals.
5. **Provides a Measure of Success:** A vision provides a measure of success. It helps individuals, organizations, and society to

evaluate their progress and determine whether they are on track to achieve their goals.

In summary, having a clear and compelling vision is critical for success in any endeavor. It provides direction, purpose, and inspiration, and helps to align efforts towards a common goal.

Once you have a clear and compelling vision, it's important to **set goals that align with that vision.** Setting goals that are aligned with your vision helps to ensure that you are working towards the bigger picture and moving in the right direction.

Here are some steps to help you set goals that align with your vision:

1. **Review your vision:** Start by reviewing your vision statement and making sure that it is still relevant and meaningful. If necessary, make adjustments to your vision to ensure that it is aligned with your current goals and aspirations.
2. **Break down your vision into smaller goals:** Once you have a clear vision, break it down into smaller, more manageable goals. These goals should be specific, measurable, achievable, relevant, and time-bound (SMART).
3. **Prioritize your goals:** Prioritize your goals based on their importance and the impact they will have on your vision. Identify the goals that are most critical to achieving your vision and focus on those first.
4. **Create an action plan:** Once you have your goals prioritized, create an action plan to achieve them. Break down the steps required to achieve each goal and assign responsibilities and timelines.
5. **Monitor progress:** Regularly monitor your progress towards achieving your goals. This will help you to identify any issues or challenges early on and make adjustments as needed.

By setting goals that align with your vision, you are more likely to achieve your long-term objectives. Remember to regularly review your vision and goals and make adjustments as necessary to ensure that you stay on track.

**Communicating your vision and goals to your team** is essential to ensure that everyone is aligned and working towards the same objectives.

Here are some steps to help you effectively communicate your vision and goals to your team:

1. **Start with your vision:** Begin by clearly articulating your vision to your team. Explain why this vision is important, what it means for the organization or team, and how everyone can contribute to its achievement.
2. **Break down the goals:** Next, break down the goals that support the vision and explain how each goal contributes to the overall vision. Make sure each goal is specific, measurable, achievable, relevant, and time-bound (SMART), and communicate this to your team.
3. **Explain the benefits:** Help your team understand the benefits of achieving the vision and goals. Explain how it will positively impact the team, the organization, and potentially the customers or stakeholders.
4. **Encourage participation:** Encourage your team to participate in the goal-setting process. Ask for feedback and suggestions on how to achieve the goals and encourage your team members to take ownership of their individual roles in achieving the goals.
5. **Establish accountability:** Establish accountability by assigning specific responsibilities and timelines for each goal.

Regularly check in with your team to monitor progress and provide feedback.

6. **Encourage open communication:** Encourage open communication and create a culture where team members feel comfortable sharing their ideas, concerns, and feedback. This will help to ensure that everyone is working towards the same goals and that any issues or challenges are addressed quickly.

In summary, communicating your vision and goals to your team is essential to ensure alignment and working towards common objectives. By following these steps, you can effectively communicate your vision and goals to your team and establish a culture of accountability, ownership, and open communication.

**Effective decision-making** is a critical skill for leaders. Leaders are responsible for making decisions that impact their team, organization, and stakeholders, and they must be able to make the right decisions consistently to achieve their goals.

Here are some reasons why effective decision making is important in leadership:

1. **Achieve objectives:** Effective decision-making helps leaders achieve their objectives. By making the right decisions, leaders can move their team or organization in the right direction, achieve goals efficiently, and maximize results.
2. **Build trust:** Effective decision-making helps build trust with team members and stakeholders. When leaders consistently make the right decisions, team members and stakeholders are more likely to trust their leadership and feel confident in their ability to lead.
3. **Manage risk:** Effective decision-making helps leaders manage risk. By considering different options and potential outcomes, leaders can make informed decisions that minimize risk and avoid negative consequences.
4. **Improve collaboration:** Effective decision making improves collaboration. Leaders who involve their team members in the decision-making process can build consensus, improve buy-in, and ensure that everyone is aligned and working towards a common goal.
5. **Enhance innovation:** Effective decision making enhances

innovation. Leaders who encourage creativity and innovation can make informed decisions that drive change, create new opportunities, and inspire growth.

In summary, effective decision making is critical for leaders to achieve their objectives, build trust, manage risk, improve collaboration, and enhance innovation. Leaders who can make the right decisions consistently, involving their team members in the process, are more likely to achieve success and maximize results.

**Making better decisions** is essential for success in personal and professional life. Here are some techniques for making better decisions:

1. **Identify the problem:** Start by clearly identifying the problem or situation that requires a decision. Clearly defining the problem will help you to focus on what is important.
2. **Gather information:** Gather as much information as possible about the situation. This may involve researching, talking to experts, or consulting with others who have experience in the area.
3. **Analyze the information:** Analyze the information you have gathered and identify the key factors that are relevant to the decision. Consider the potential risks, benefits, and consequences of each option.
4. **Consider multiple options:** Consider multiple options and evaluate each option based on the key factors you have identified. Try to think creatively and outside the box to come up with innovative solutions.
5. **Seek feedback:** Seek feedback from others who may be affected by the decision or who have experience in the area. Consider their perspectives and incorporate their feedback into the decision-making process.
6. **Make a decision:** Based on the information you have gathered and analyzed, make a decision that is well-informed and aligned with your goals.

7. **Evaluate the decision:** After making a decision, evaluate the outcome and determine whether the decision was successful or not. This will help you to learn from your decision-making process and improve your skills for future decisions.

In addition to these techniques, it's important to stay calm, rational, and objective when making decisions. Avoid making decisions based on emotions or personal biases and try to remain focused on the facts and evidence.

In summary, making better decisions requires a systematic and well-informed approach that involves identifying the problem, gathering information, analyzing the information, considering multiple options, seeking feedback, making a decision, and evaluating the decision. By following these techniques, you can improve your decision-making skills and make better decisions in your personal and professional life.

**Intuition** can play an important role in decision-making as it allows us to make quick judgments based on past experiences, knowledge, and instincts, without necessarily relying on explicit reasoning or analysis. Intuitive decision-making can be particularly useful in situations where time is a critical factor, or where there is incomplete or ambiguous information.

However, it's important to note that intuition is not infallible, and relying too heavily on intuition without proper analysis or evaluation can lead to biases and errors in judgment. Intuitive decision-making can also be influenced by a range of factors such as emotions, personal biases, and cognitive heuristics.

Therefore, while intuition can be a valuable tool in decision-making, it should be used in conjunction with other decision-making strategies, such as logical analysis and evaluation of available information, to ensure that the decision is well-informed and rational.

**Delegation** is a critical skill for effective leadership. Delegation involves assigning tasks, responsibilities, and authority to others, and it is an essential aspect of managing a team or organization.

There are several reasons why delegation is important in leadership:

1. **Effective use of resources:** Delegation helps leaders to make the most effective use of available resources, including time, expertise, and manpower. By delegating tasks to others, leaders can free up their own time and focus on high-level strategic planning and decision-making.
2. **Empowerment and development:** Delegating tasks helps to empower team members by providing them with autonomy and ownership over their work. This can foster a sense of responsibility and accountability, and it can help team members to develop new skills and knowledge.
3. **Improved efficiency and productivity:** Delegation can help to improve efficiency and productivity by allowing tasks to be completed more quickly and effectively. By delegating tasks to team members who have the appropriate skills and expertise, leaders can ensure that tasks are completed to a high standard and in a timely manner.
4. **Building trust and relationships:** Delegation can help to build trust and relationships between leaders and their team members. By demonstrating trust in their team members' abilities, leaders can foster a culture of mutual respect and collaboration.

Overall, delegation is a critical skill for effective leadership. By delegating tasks and responsibilities, leaders can empower their team members, improve efficiency and productivity, and build trust and relationships within their team.

**Effective delegation** requires careful planning, communication, and follow-up. Here are some techniques for effective delegation:

1. **Identify tasks to delegate:** Start by identifying tasks that can be delegated to others. Consider the tasks that are time-consuming, routine, or can be completed by someone with the appropriate skills and expertise.
2. **Select the right person for the task:** When delegating tasks, it's important to select the right person for the job. Consider the skills, expertise, and availability of team members when deciding whom to delegate tasks to.
3. **Communicate clearly:** When delegating tasks, it's important to communicate clearly about what is expected, including deadlines, quality standards, and any other relevant information. Be sure to provide clear instructions and answer any questions that team members may have.
4. **Provide resources and support:** Ensure that team members have the resources and support they need to complete the task successfully. This may include access to information, tools, and training.
5. **Monitor progress and provide feedback:** Check in with team members regularly to monitor progress and provide feedback. This can help to ensure that the task is proceeding as planned and can provide an opportunity to make any necessary adjustments.
6. **Recognize success:** Finally, be sure to recognize and reward team members for their efforts and successes. This can help

to build motivation, morale, and a sense of accomplishment.

Overall, effective delegation requires careful planning, communication, and follow-up. By following these techniques, leaders can ensure that tasks are completed efficiently and effectively while empowering their team members to grow and develop their skills.

**Delegating tasks is an important skill for effective leadership,** but it can be easy to make mistakes if not done properly. Here are some common delegation mistakes to avoid:

1. **Failing to communicate expectations:** One of the most common delegation mistakes is failing to communicate clear expectations to team members. This can lead to confusion, misunderstandings, and ultimately, poor performance.
2. **Not delegating enough:** Some leaders may feel that it's easier to do everything themselves rather than delegate tasks to others. However, this can lead to burnout and a lack of productivity.
3. **Micromanaging:** Another common mistake is micromanaging team members when delegating tasks. This can be demotivating for team members and can lead to decreased productivity.
4. **Failing to provide adequate support:** Leaders may delegate tasks without providing adequate support, such as training or resources, which can lead to frustration and poor performance.
5. **Not providing feedback:** Leaders may fail to provide timely and constructive feedback to team members, which can prevent them from learning and improving.
6. **Not recognizing success:** Finally, leaders may fail to recognize and reward team members for their successes, which can lead to demotivation and reduced morale.

Overall, effective delegation requires clear communication, trust, and support. By avoiding these common delegation mistakes, leaders can empower their team members to grow and develop their skills while achieving the desired results.

There are several **different types of teams** that organizations may use to accomplish their goals. Here are some of the most common types of teams:

1. **Functional Teams:** These teams are composed of individuals who have similar skills and knowledge and work together on a specific function or department within an organization, such as marketing or finance.
2. **Cross-functional Teams:** These teams are composed of individuals from different departments or functions within an organization who work together to accomplish a specific goal or project.
3. **Self-managed Teams:** These teams are composed of individuals who work together to complete a specific task or project without a designated leader. Instead, the team members collectively manage the work and make decisions.
4. **Virtual Teams:** These teams are composed of individuals who work together from different locations and communicate primarily through technology, such as email, video conferencing, or online collaboration tools.
5. **Project Teams:** These teams are formed to work on a specific project, typically for a defined period of time. Project teams may include individuals from different departments or functions and may disband once the project is completed.
6. **Problem-solving Teams:** These teams are formed to address a specific problem or challenge within an organization. They may be composed of individuals from

different departments or functions and work together to identify and implement a solution.

Overall, the type of team that an organization uses will depend on its specific needs and goals. Each type of team has its own strengths and weaknesses, and organizations may use a combination of different teams to achieve their objectives.

**Building and leading an effective team** requires a combination of several techniques, including:

1. **Clarify team goals and expectations:** Ensure that everyone on the team understands the team's goals, roles, and responsibilities. Set clear expectations for the team's performance and communicate these expectations regularly.
2. **Encourage open communication:** Create an environment where team members feel comfortable sharing their ideas, concerns, and feedback. Encourage active listening and respectful communication.
3. **Foster collaboration:** Encourage team members to work together, share their skills and knowledge, and support each other. Foster a team culture that values collaboration and teamwork.
4. **Lead by example:** As a leader, model the behavior you want to see in your team. Show respect, honesty, and integrity. Be willing to admit when you make a mistake and use it as an opportunity to learn and grow.
5. **Provide feedback and recognition:** Regularly provide feedback to your team members, both individually and as a group. Recognize and reward their achievements and contributions.
6. **Develop your team members:** Provide opportunities for your team members to develop their skills and knowledge. Encourage them to take on new challenges and responsibilities.

7. **Manage conflicts effectively:** Conflicts are inevitable in any team, but it's important to manage them effectively. Encourage open communication, listen to all perspectives, and work together to find a resolution that everyone can support.
8. **Celebrate successes:** Celebrate your team's successes together. Acknowledge the hard work and contributions of each team member and recognize the impact of the team's achievements.

By implementing these techniques, you can build and lead a highly effective team that achieves its goals and delivers results.

**Diversity plays a significant role in team dynamics.** A diverse team is one that consists of members with different backgrounds, experiences, perspectives, and skills. These differences can bring unique insights, creativity, and problem-solving abilities to a team, leading to better decision-making and improved outcomes.

Here are some ways in which diversity can impact team dynamics:

1. **Different perspectives:** Members of a diverse team bring a variety of perspectives to the table, which can lead to more creative solutions and better problem-solving. When team members come from different backgrounds, they are more likely to have unique perspectives and experiences that can help the team approach problems in new and innovative ways.
2. **Increased creativity:** A diverse team can lead to increased creativity because it allows for a wider range of ideas to be generated. When people with different backgrounds and experiences collaborate, they can come up with new and innovative solutions to problems.
3. **Improved communication:** In a diverse team, members must learn to communicate effectively with people from different backgrounds and cultures. This can lead to improved communication skills and more effective collaboration.
4. **Reduced groupthink:** Groupthink occurs when members of a team conform to the opinions and ideas of the group,

rather than expressing their own opinions. In a diverse team, members are less likely to conform to the group's opinions, which can lead to more diverse and innovative ideas.

5. **Increased empathy:** Working with people from diverse backgrounds can increase empathy and understanding of different perspectives and experiences. This can lead to a more inclusive and supportive team environment.

Overall, diversity can have a positive impact on team dynamics by bringing together different perspectives, skills, and experiences to achieve better results. It is important for team leaders to recognize the value of diversity and actively foster an inclusive team environment.

**Motivation and inspiration** are critical components of effective leadership. A motivated and inspired team is likely to be more productive, creative, and engaged in their work, leading to better organizational outcomes.

Motivation refers to the factors that drive an individual to take action or achieve a goal. Leaders who are able to motivate their team members can inspire them to work towards a common goal, overcome challenges, and achieve success. Motivation can take many forms, including financial incentives, recognition, opportunities for growth and development, and a positive work environment.

Inspiration, on the other hand, is about creating a sense of purpose and direction for the team. When leaders are able to inspire their team members, they can help them connect with the bigger picture, understand the importance of their work, and feel a sense of fulfillment and meaning in what they do. This can lead to increased engagement, commitment, and loyalty from team members.

Leaders who are able to effectively motivate and inspire their team members can create a culture of high performance, where team members are driven to achieve their best work. This can result in better outcomes for the organization, including increased productivity, higher quality work, and greater innovation.

In summary, motivation, and inspiration are critical components of effective leadership, and leaders who are able to harness these factors can create a high-performing team that drives organizational success.

There are many techniques that leaders can use to motivate and inspire their team members. Here are some effective techniques:

1. **Set clear goals and expectations:** Providing clear goals and expectations can give team members a sense of purpose and direction. When goals are specific, measurable, achievable, relevant, and time-bound (SMART), team members can understand what is expected of them and can work towards achieving those goals.
2. **Provide regular feedback:** Regular feedback can help team members understand what they are doing well and where they can improve. Feedback can be both positive and constructive and should be given in a timely and specific manner.
3. **Recognize and reward achievements:** Recognizing and rewarding team members for their achievements can help them feel valued and appreciated. Rewards can take many forms, including financial incentives, public recognition, and opportunities for growth and development.
4. **Create a positive work environment:** A positive work environment can help team members feel motivated and engaged. Leaders can create a positive work environment by fostering open communication, providing opportunities for collaboration and teamwork, and promoting work-life balance.
5. **Lead by example:** Leaders who lead by example can inspire their team members to follow their lead. When leaders demonstrate the values and behaviors they expect from their team members, they can create a culture of accountability and high performance.
6. **Provide opportunities for growth and development:** Providing opportunities for growth and development can help team members feel motivated and engaged. Leaders

can provide opportunities for training, mentoring, and career advancement to help team members develop their skills and achieve their goals.

7. **Communicate a compelling vision:** Communicating a compelling vision can inspire team members to work towards a common goal. Leaders can communicate a vision that is meaningful and inspiring, and that aligns with the values and purpose of the organization.

By using these techniques, leaders can motivate and inspire their team members to achieve their best work and drive organizational success.

While motivation is a critical component of effective leadership, there are **some common pitfalls that leaders should avoid** in order to maintain a motivated and engaged team.

Here are some common motivation pitfalls to avoid:

1. **Ignoring individual needs:** Leaders who ignore the individual needs of their team members may struggle to motivate and engage them. It's important to understand that everyone is motivated by different things, and leaders should take the time to get to know their team members and what motivates them.
2. **Focusing only on short-term goals:** While short-term goals can be motivating, leaders who only focus on short-term goals may struggle to maintain motivation over the long term. It's important to balance short-term goals with a long-term vision that can provide a sense of purpose and direction.
3. **Ignoring feedback:** Leaders who ignore feedback from their team members may struggle to maintain motivation and engagement. It's important to listen to feedback and take action to address any concerns or issues.
4. **Failing to recognize achievements:** Leaders who fail to recognize the achievements of their team members may struggle to maintain motivation and engagement. It's important to celebrate successes and recognize the hard work and contributions of team members.

5. **Micromanaging:** Leaders who micromanage their team members may struggle to maintain motivation and engagement. Micromanaging can create a sense of mistrust and can make team members feel undervalued and disengaged.
6. **Providing insufficient resources:** Leaders who do not provide sufficient resources, including time, budget, and personnel, may struggle to maintain motivation and engagement. It's important to ensure that team members have the resources they need to do their jobs effectively.
7. **Failing to lead by example:** Leaders who fail to lead by example may struggle to maintain motivation and engagement. It's important to demonstrate the values and behaviors that are expected of team members.

By avoiding these common motivation pitfalls, leaders can maintain a motivated and engaged team that is focused on achieving its goals and driving organizational success.

**Effective conflict resolution** is a critical component of leadership. Conflict can arise in any workplace, and if not handled effectively, it can lead to decreased productivity, low morale, and a toxic work environment. Leaders who are able to effectively resolve conflicts can help create a positive and productive work environment, where team members are able to work together to achieve their goals.

Here are some reasons why effective conflict resolution is important in leadership:

1. **Increased productivity:** When conflicts are not effectively resolved, they can lead to decreased productivity as team members become distracted and disengaged. Leaders who are able to resolve conflicts quickly and effectively can help team members stay focused on their work, leading to increased productivity.
2. **Improved communication:** Conflict can often arise due to miscommunication or misunderstandings. Leaders who are able to effectively resolve conflicts can help improve communication between team members, leading to better collaboration and teamwork.
3. **Higher morale:** Conflicts can create a negative work environment, leading to low morale and high turnover. Leaders who are able to resolve conflicts in a positive and constructive manner can help create a positive work environment, leading to higher morale and greater job satisfaction.

4. **Better problem-solving:** Conflict resolution often involves problem-solving. Leaders who are able to effectively resolve conflicts can help team members develop their problem-solving skills, leading to better decision-making and improved outcomes.
5. **Stronger relationships:** When conflicts are effectively resolved, it can lead to stronger relationships between team members. Leaders who are able to facilitate conflict resolution can help team members build trust and respect for one another, leading to stronger relationships and a stronger team.

In summary, effective conflict resolution is a critical component of leadership. Leaders who are able to resolve conflicts quickly and effectively can help create a positive and productive work environment, leading to increased productivity, improved communication, higher morale, better problem-solving, and stronger relationships between team members.

Conflicts can arise in various situations, whether it's at work, in relationships, or in other areas of life.

**Here are some techniques that can help resolve conflicts:**

1. **Active listening:** When trying to resolve a conflict, it's important to actively listen to the other person's perspective without interrupting or dismissing their feelings. This involves paying attention to their words, body language, and tone of voice.
2. **Empathy:** Try to understand the other person's point of view and feelings. Acknowledge their emotions and show that you understand their perspective. This can help build trust and create an environment for productive problem-solving.
3. **Communication:** Be clear and concise when communicating your own perspective and feelings. Use "I" statements to describe how you feel, rather than placing blame on the other person.
4. **Collaboration:** Work together with the other person to find a mutually beneficial solution. Brainstorm ideas and be open to compromise.
5. **Mediation:** If the conflict is particularly complex or emotionally charged, it may be helpful to bring in a third-party mediator to facilitate the discussion and help guide the resolution process.
6. **Taking a break:** If emotions are running high, it may be

necessary to take a break from the discussion to cool down and gather your thoughts.

Remember, conflict resolution is about finding a solution that is acceptable to both parties. It often requires compromise and a willingness to work together to find a resolution.

**Empathy** is a critical component of conflict resolution because it helps people to understand and relate to the feelings and perspectives of others involved in the conflict. When people feel that their emotions and perspectives are being listened to and understood, they are more likely to be open to finding a mutually beneficial solution.

Empathy allows people to put themselves in the other person's shoes and see the situation from their perspective. This can help to reduce defensiveness and create a more cooperative and understanding environment. When people feel heard and understood, they are more likely to be open to considering different viewpoints and options for resolution.

Empathy can also help to de-escalate emotions that are often associated with conflict, such as anger, frustration, and resentment. When someone feels that their emotions are being acknowledged and validated, they are often more willing to work towards finding a solution that is acceptable to both parties.

Overall, empathy plays a crucial role in conflict resolution by promoting understanding, cooperation, and a willingness to find common ground. By demonstrating empathy and actively listening to the perspectives of others, people can create a more positive and productive environment for resolving conflicts.

**Effective time management** is a critical component of leadership because it helps leaders to prioritize their tasks, manage their workload, and achieve their goals in a timely manner.

Here are some reasons why time management is important in leadership:

1. **Maximizing productivity:** Leaders are often responsible for managing multiple tasks and projects, and effective time management allows them to prioritize their workload and focus on the most important tasks. This helps to maximize productivity and ensure that the most critical tasks are completed within the required timeframe.
2. **Meeting deadlines:** Time management enables leaders to plan their work and allocate their time effectively, ensuring that they can meet deadlines and deliver results on time. This is particularly important in fast-paced environments where deadlines are tight and failure to meet them can have significant consequences.
3. **Managing stress:** Poor time management can lead to stress and overwhelm, which can negatively impact a leader's ability to make sound decisions and communicate effectively. By effectively managing their time, leaders can reduce stress and maintain a clear and focused mindset.
4. **Building trust and credibility:** Effective time management shows that leaders are organized, reliable, and committed to meeting their responsibilities. This helps to build trust and

credibility with team members, stakeholders, and other stakeholders.

5. **Creating a culture of efficiency:** When leaders prioritize time management, they set an example for their team members and create a culture of efficiency and productivity. This can help to improve team morale and create a more positive and motivated work environment.

In short, effective time management is a critical skill for leaders to master in order to achieve their goals, build trust and credibility, and create a positive and productive work environment.

Here are some techniques for managing your time more effectively:

1. **Prioritize tasks:** Make a list of all the tasks that need to be completed, then prioritize them based on their importance and urgency. This will help you to focus on the most critical tasks first, ensuring that you make progress on the most important items.
2. **Set goals:** Identify specific goals that you want to achieve and set deadlines for them. This helps to keep you focused and motivated and ensures that you are working towards specific outcomes.
3. **Use a calendar:** Use a calendar to schedule your time and assign specific blocks of time for different tasks. This helps to ensure that you are using your time efficiently and that you are allocating enough time for each task.
4. **Limit distractions:** Identify the things that distract you, such as social media, emails, or phone calls. Limit these

distractions by turning off notifications, setting specific times to check email, or using apps to block distracting websites.

5. **Delegate tasks:** Identify tasks that can be delegated to others and assign them to appropriate team members. This helps to free up your time and allows you to focus on tasks that require your specific skills and expertise.
6. **Take breaks:** Taking breaks can help to improve productivity and reduce stress. Schedule regular breaks throughout your day to recharge and refocus.
7. **Learn to say no:** If you are already overwhelmed with tasks, it's important to learn to say no to additional requests. This helps to manage your workload and ensure that you are not taking on too much at once.

Overall, effective time management requires a combination of planning, prioritization, and focus. By implementing these techniques, you can manage your time more effectively and achieve your goals with greater efficiency and less stress.

**Burnout** is a state of emotional, physical, and mental exhaustion that can result from prolonged stress and overwork. Here are some tips for avoiding burnout:

1. **Set realistic goals:** It's important to set realistic goals that are achievable within a reasonable timeframe. Unrealistic goals can lead to stress and burnout, as you may feel that you are constantly falling short of expectations.
2. **Prioritize self-care:** Make time for self-care activities such as exercise, meditation, or spending time with loved ones. This helps to reduce stress and maintain a healthy work-life balance.
3. **Take breaks:** Regular breaks throughout the day can help to reduce stress and prevent burnout. Take short breaks to stretch, walk around, or engage in other activities that help you to recharge.
4. **Manage your workload:** Try to manage your workload by prioritizing tasks, delegating responsibilities, and setting boundaries. Don't take on too much at once, and don't be afraid to say no to additional requests.
5. **Seek support:** Reach out to colleagues, friends, or family members for support when you are feeling overwhelmed. This can help you to process your feelings and get the support you need to manage stress and prevent burnout.
6. **Practice mindfulness:** Mindfulness techniques such as meditation or deep breathing can help to reduce stress and improve focus. Incorporate these techniques into your daily

routine to help manage stress and increase resilience.

7. **Take time off:** If you are feeling burned out, it may be necessary to take time off from work to recharge and regroup. Use your vacation time or take a personal day to rest and relax.

Overall, preventing burnout requires a combination of self-care, stress management, and support. By prioritizing your well-being and taking proactive steps to manage stress, you can avoid burnout and maintain a healthy work-life balance.

**Continuous learning and growth** are essential for effective leadership. Leaders who commit to ongoing learning are better equipped to adapt to change, make informed decisions, and inspire their teams to achieve their goals.

Leaders who prioritize continuous learning and growth are more likely to stay up to date with industry trends, innovations, and emerging technologies. This allows them to make informed decisions that can improve the performance of their team or organization. Additionally, leaders who are committed to personal growth are more likely to develop a growth mindset, which enables them to approach challenges as opportunities for learning and development.

Furthermore, continuous learning and growth can help leaders cultivate a culture of learning within their organization. When leaders prioritize learning, they set an example for their team members, who are more likely to follow suit. This creates a culture of continuous improvement that can help organizations stay competitive in a rapidly changing marketplace.

Overall, continuous learning and growth are critical for effective leadership. Leaders who prioritize learning and growth are better equipped to adapt to change, make informed decisions, inspire their teams, and create a culture of learning within their organizations.

There are several techniques that can help you develop your skills and knowledge:

1. **Continuous learning:** Make learning a habit by reading books, attending seminars and workshops, taking online

courses, or enrolling in formal education programs. This will help you stay up to date with the latest industry trends and developments.

2. **Mentorship:** Seek out a mentor who has experience in your field and can guide you in your career development. A mentor can provide valuable advice, feedback, and support to help you grow and develop your skills.
3. **Networking:** Connect with other professionals in your field through professional associations, conferences, and social media platforms. Networking can help you develop new skills and gain insights into best practices in your industry.
4. **Practice:** Practice your skills regularly to develop mastery. Whether it's through simulations, role-playing exercises, or real-life situations, practice can help you refine your skills and gain confidence in your abilities.
5. **Feedback:** Seek feedback from colleagues, supervisors, and mentors to identify areas for improvement and build on your strengths. Constructive feedback can help you learn from your mistakes and make progress in your career.
6. **Self-reflection:** Take time to reflect on your experiences, successes, and challenges. Self-reflection can help you identify areas for improvement and set goals for your personal and professional development.

By incorporating these techniques into your daily routine, you can develop your skills and knowledge, and achieve your career goals.

**Mentorship** plays a crucial role in leadership development. A mentor is an experienced professional who provides guidance, support, and feedback to a less experienced individual in their field. Mentorship can help emerging leaders develop the skills and knowledge needed to succeed in their roles, while also providing them with a role model to emulate.

Here are some ways mentorship can support leadership development:

1. **Guidance and support:** A mentor can provide guidance and support to an emerging leader as they navigate their career path. This can include advice on career goals, professional development opportunities, and strategies for overcoming challenges.
2. **Skill development:** A mentor can help an emerging leader develop specific skills that are essential for success in their role. This can include communication, problem-solving, decision-making, and conflict-resolution skills.
3. **Networking:** A mentor can introduce an emerging leader to other professionals in their field, helping them to expand their network and build relationships that can be valuable throughout their career.
4. **Role modeling:** A mentor can serve as a role model for an emerging leader, demonstrating effective leadership behaviors and strategies. This can help the emerging leader develop their own leadership style and approach.

5. **Feedback:** A mentor can provide feedback to an emerging leader on their performance and progress, helping them to identify areas for improvement and build on their strengths.

Overall, mentorship is a valuable tool for leadership development. By providing guidance, support, skill development, networking opportunities, role modeling, and feedback, a mentor can help an emerging leader grow and develop their leadership abilities.

**Leadership** is a complex and multifaceted concept that is essential for success in all areas of life. Effective leadership requires a combination of skills, including communication, problem-solving, decision-making, and emotional intelligence. It also involves the ability to inspire and motivate others, build relationships, and navigate change and uncertainty.

One of the key characteristics of effective leadership is a commitment to continuous learning and growth. Leaders who prioritize personal and professional development are better equipped to adapt to change, make informed decisions, and inspire their teams to achieve their goals. Mentorship, networking, and ongoing learning opportunities are all valuable tools for leadership development.

Leadership is not only about achieving individual success but also about creating a positive impact on others and the world around us. Effective leaders prioritize the well-being and success of their team members, customers, and communities, and strive to make a positive difference in the world through their actions and decisions.

In conclusion, leadership is a critical skill that can be developed and honed through ongoing learning, mentorship, and practice. Effective leaders prioritize personal and professional growth, inspire, and motivate others, and create a positive impact on their teams, organizations, and communities.

Part Two

# THE SALES MANAGEMENT TOOLKIT

**Sales management** is the process of planning, organizing, directing, and controlling the activities and personnel involved in the sales function of a business. The role of a sales manager is to lead and direct a team of salespeople toward achieving the sales targets and objectives set by the organization.

To be successful in this role, a sales manager needs to possess a variety of skills and tools. Here are some of the key skills and tools that are essential for sales managers to succeed:

1. **Leadership skills:** Sales managers must have strong leadership skills to motivate their team, provide direction and guidance, and create a positive and productive work environment.
2. **Communication skills:** A sales manager must be an effective communicator to convey sales goals and objectives, provide feedback, and ensure that everyone is working towards a common goal.
3. **Sales expertise:** Knowledge of the sales process, including prospecting, lead generation, sales presentations, and closing techniques, is crucial for a sales manager to coach and mentor their team effectively.
4. **Analytical skills:** Sales managers need to be able to analyze sales data and market trends to identify opportunities, develop strategies, and make informed decisions.
5. **CRM software:** Customer Relationship Management (CRM) software is an essential tool for sales managers to manage customer interactions, track sales activities, and

generate reports to monitor progress and performance.

6. **Training and development programs:** Sales managers need to develop and implement training programs to help their team improve their sales skills and stay up to date with industry trends and best practices.
7. **Time management and organization**: Sales managers must be able to prioritize tasks, manage their time effectively, and stay organized to ensure that sales goals are met.

In summary, the role of a sales manager is to lead and direct a team of salespeople toward achieving the sales targets and objectives set by the organization. To succeed in this role, sales managers need to possess a variety of skills and tools, including leadership skills, communication skills, sales expertise, analytical skills, CRM software, training and development programs, and time management and organization skills.

As a sales manager, having a deep understanding of your target market is essential to developing **effective sales strategies and achieving sales goals.** Market research is a critical component of understanding your market and identifying customer needs. Here are some market research techniques and strategies for **identifying customer needs:**

1. **Surveys:** Surveys are a common and effective way to gather information about customer needs and preferences. Surveys can be conducted online, via email, or in person and can be designed to collect quantitative or qualitative data.
2. **Focus Groups:** Focus groups are small groups of individuals who are brought together to provide feedback on a product, service, or idea. Focus groups allow you to gather qualitative data and gain insights into customer needs and preferences.
3. **Social Media Listening:** Social media platforms provide a wealth of data on customer needs and preferences. Social media listening involves monitoring social media channels for customer feedback and insights.
4. **Competitor Analysis:** Analyzing your competitors can provide valuable insights into customer needs and preferences. By understanding what your competitors are doing well and where they are falling short, you can identify opportunities to differentiate your product or service.
5. **Customer Interviews:** Customer interviews involve one-on-one conversations with customers to gain insights into

their needs and preferences. Customer interviews can be conducted in person or over the phone and can provide valuable qualitative data.

6. **Data Analysis:** Analyzing sales data, website analytics, and other quantitative data can provide insights into customer behavior and preferences. By analyzing this data, you can identify trends and patterns that can inform your sales strategies.

In summary, market research is a critical component of understanding your target market and identifying customer needs. Techniques and strategies for market research include surveys, focus groups, social media listening, competitor analysis, customer interviews, and data analysis. By leveraging these techniques and strategies, sales managers can gain valuable insights into their target market and develop effective sales strategies that meet customer needs and drive sales growth.

**Building a successful sales team** is crucial to the growth and success of any business. Here are some steps to finding, hiring, and training top-performing sales professionals:

1. **Define your ideal candidate**: Before you start the hiring process, it's important to define the skills, experience, and personality traits you're looking for in a sales professional. This will help you identify the right candidates and ensure that they are a good fit for your organization.
2. **Source candidates:** There are many ways to source candidates, including job boards, LinkedIn, industry events, and referrals from current employees or industry contacts. Consider using multiple channels to maximize your reach and attract a diverse pool of candidates.
3. **Screen candidates:** Once you've identified potential candidates, conduct phone or video interviews to screen them for the skills and experience you're looking for. This will help you narrow down your list of candidates and identify those who are most qualified for the role.
4. **Conduct in-person interviews**: Invite top candidates for in-person interviews to assess their fit with your organization and team culture. Use behavioral interviewing techniques to assess their skills, experience, and personality traits.
5. **Make an offer:** Once you've identified the right candidate, make an offer that is competitive with the market and includes clear expectations for performance and compensation.

6. **Train and onboard:** Once you've hired your sales team, provide comprehensive training and onboarding to ensure that they have the skills, knowledge, and tools they need to succeed. This may include product and market training, sales process training, and ongoing coaching and development.
7. **Provide ongoing support:** To ensure the ongoing success of your sales team, provide them with ongoing support and resources, including sales tools and technology, ongoing training and development, and regular feedback and coaching.

In summary, building a successful sales team requires a clear understanding of the skills and experience you're looking for, sourcing candidates through multiple channels, conducting thorough screening and interviewing, making competitive offers, providing comprehensive training, and onboarding, and providing ongoing support and resources. By following these steps, you can build a top-performing sales team that drives growth and success for your business.

A successful **sales strategy** is essential for achieving your business goals. Here are some key elements of a successful sales strategy and how to implement it effectively:

1. **Define your sales goals:** The first step in developing a sales strategy is to define your sales goals. This includes setting targets for revenue, sales volume, and market share. Your sales goals should align with your overall business goals and be specific, measurable, achievable, relevant, and time bound.
2. **Identify your target market:** Once you've defined your sales goals, you need to identify your target market. This includes understanding your ideal customer profile, the needs and pain points of your customers, and the buying process for your product or service.
3. **Develop a unique value proposition:** Your unique value proposition is what sets you apart from your competitors and makes your product or service compelling to your target market. Develop a clear and concise value proposition that communicates the benefits of your product or service to your customers.
4. **Develop a sales process:** A sales process is a series of steps that your sales team follows to convert leads into customers. Develop a sales process that is aligned with your target market and unique value proposition. This should include lead generation, qualification, discovery, presentation, objection handling, closing, and follow-up.

5. **Define sales roles and responsibilities:** To implement your sales strategy effectively, you need to define sales roles and responsibilities. This includes identifying the skills and experience required for each role, setting clear expectations for performance, and providing ongoing feedback and coaching.
6. **Use technology and data:** Technology and data can help you optimize your sales strategy and improve your sales performance. Use customer relationship management (CRM) software to manage your sales process, track customer interactions, and generate reports. Use sales analytics to track sales performance, identify trends, and optimize your sales strategy.
7. **Continuously improve:** A successful sales strategy requires continuous improvement. This includes monitoring your sales performance metrics, analyzing data, and making adjustments to your sales process and strategy as needed.
8. **Define your business objectives:** Before you can start forecasting sales and creating a budget, you need to have a clear understanding of your business objectives. What are your short-term and long-term goals? What do you hope to achieve with your business? Having a clear understanding of your objectives will help you to develop a sales forecast and budget that will help you to achieve those goals.
9. **Analyze historical sales data:** To create an accurate sales forecast, you should analyze historical sales data to identify patterns and trends. Look at your sales figures from previous years, as well as any seasonal variations or fluctuations that may have affected your sales.
10. **Consider market trends:** Your sales forecast should also

take into account any market trends or changes that may affect your business. For example, if there is increased competition in your industry, you may need to adjust your sales forecast accordingly.

11. **Set realistic sales goals:** Based on your historical sales data and market trends, you can set realistic sales goals for your business. These goals should be specific, measurable, and achievable, and should align with your overall business objectives.
12. **Develop a sales budget:** Once you have a sales forecast, you can develop a sales budget that outlines your projected revenue and expenses for the coming year. Your budget should include all of your sales-related expenses, such as marketing and advertising costs, as well as any other expenses that are directly related to generating sales.
13. **Monitor and adjust your forecast and budget:** Your sales forecast and budget should be reviewed and adjusted regularly to ensure they remain aligned with your business objectives. Monitor your sales figures and adjust your forecast and budget as necessary to ensure your business stays on track.

By following these steps, you can develop a sales forecast and budget that aligns with your business objectives and helps you to achieve your goals.

Here are some key indicators and areas of improvement for the performance of sales managers:

1. **Sales Revenue:** This is the most basic and important metric to track. It shows the total amount of revenue generated by your sales team. Sales managers should track revenue on a daily, weekly, monthly, and yearly basis to gain insights into their team's performance.
2. **Sales Growth:** This metric measures the percentage increase or decrease in sales revenue over a specific period of time. Sales managers should track sales growth to identify trends and patterns in their team's performance over time.
3. **Conversion Rate:** This measures the percentage of leads that are converted into customers. Sales managers should track the conversion rate to identify areas where their team may need additional training or support.
4. **Average Deal Size:** This metric measures the average value of each sale. Sales managers should track this metric to identify opportunities to increase revenue by upselling or cross-selling.
5. **Sales Cycle Length:** This measures the time it takes for a lead to become a customer. Sales managers should track this metric to identify bottlenecks in their sales process and find ways to streamline it.
6. **Sales Pipeline Velocity:** This metric measures the speed at which leads move through the sales pipeline. Sales managers should track this metric to identify areas where

their team may be losing momentum and find ways to keep leads moving through the pipeline.

7. **Salesperson Activity:** This measures the number of activities performed by each salesperson, such as calls, emails, and meetings. Sales managers should track this metric to identify their top-performing salespeople and find ways to replicate their success across the team.

By tracking these key performance indicators, sales managers can gain insights into their team's performance, identify areas for improvement, and take action to improve sales performance over time. It's important to remember that these metrics should be used to guide decision-making and not just to measure performance. Sales managers should use them to identify areas for improvement and take action to address any issues that are identified.

**Managing your sales pipeline** is essential to ensuring a steady flow of revenue and maximizing your sales results.

Here are some best practices for managing your sales pipeline:

1. **Define your sales stages:** Define the stages that a lead goes through as they move through your sales process. This helps you to track progress and identify bottlenecks in your pipeline.
2. **Qualify your leads:** Not every lead is a good fit for your product or service. Qualify your leads to ensure that you are focusing your efforts on those with the highest potential for conversion.
3. **Assign ownership:** Assign ownership of each lead to a specific salesperson, so they are responsible for moving that lead through the pipeline.
4. **Set goals:** Set goals for each stage of the pipeline to ensure that you are making progress towards your sales objectives.
5. **Monitor progress:** Monitor progress at each stage of the pipeline to identify areas where leads are getting stuck and find ways to keep them moving through the pipeline.'
6. **Analyze data:** Analyze data from your pipeline to identify trends and patterns in your sales process. Use this data to optimize your pipeline for maximum results.
7. **Use automation tools:** Use automation tools to streamline your sales process and reduce manual tasks. This allows

your sales team to focus on high-value activities like building relationships with leads.

8. **Regularly review and update your pipeline:** Regularly review and update your pipeline to ensure that it remains aligned with your business objectives and sales goals.
9. **Use a customer relationship management (CRM) system:** A CRM system can help you to manage your sales pipeline more effectively by providing a centralized platform for tracking leads, managing customer data, and automating tasks.
10. **Prioritize leads:** Prioritize your leads based on their likelihood to convert and their potential value. This helps you to focus your efforts on the leads that are most likely to drive revenue.
11. **Develop a sales playbook:** Develop a sales playbook that outlines your sales process, best practices, and key messaging points. This ensures that your sales team is aligned and consistent in their approach.
12. **Provide ongoing training:** Provide ongoing training for your sales team to ensure that they are up to date on new products, industry trends, and sales techniques.
13. **Measure and track performance:** Measure and track the performance of your sales team and individual salespeople to identify areas for improvement and provide coaching and support.
14. **Celebrate successes:** Celebrate your team's successes and achievements to build morale and motivation. This helps to create a positive sales culture and encourages your team to continue striving for success.

By implementing these best practices for managing your sales pipeline, you can optimize your sales process, increase your conversion rates, and drive revenue growth. Remember that effective pipeline management requires ongoing attention and optimization, so be sure to regularly review and update your pipeline to ensure that it remains aligned with your business objectives and sales goals.

**Lead generation** is the process of identifying potential customers who are interested in your products or services. Nurturing these leads involves building a relationship with them, providing them with relevant information, and guiding them through the sales funnel until they become paying customers.

Here are some techniques for lead generation and best practices for nurturing them through the sales funnel:

1. **Define your ideal customer:** Before you can generate leads, you need to know who your ideal customer is. This will help you target your marketing efforts more effectively.
2. **Use multiple channels for lead generation:** Don't rely on just one channel for lead generation. Use a mix of channels such as email marketing, social media, trade shows, and content marketing to reach your target audience.
3. **Create high-quality content:** Create content that provides value to your target audience. This could be in the form of blog posts, whitepapers, case studies, or videos.
4. **Offer incentives:** Offer incentives such as free trials, consultations, or demos to encourage potential customers to take the next step in the sales process.
5. **Use lead scoring:** Use lead scoring to prioritize leads based on their level of interest and engagement with your brand. This will help you focus your efforts on the most promising leads.
6. **Use marketing automation:** Use marketing automation

tools to streamline your lead nurturing process. This could include automated email campaigns, personalized content recommendations, and lead scoring.

7. **Use personalized communication:** Personalize your communication with leads based on their interests and behavior. This could include sending targeted emails or providing customized content recommendations.
8. **Provide excellent customer service:** Provide excellent customer service throughout the sales process to build trust and loyalty with your leads. This will increase the chances that they will become paying customers and refer others to your business.
9. **Use social media advertising:** Social media advertising can be an effective way to generate leads. Platforms like Facebook and LinkedIn allow you to target your ads to specific audiences based on demographics, interests, and behaviors.
10. **Attend industry events:** Attend trade shows, conferences, and other industry events to connect with potential customers and generate leads. Be sure to have a clear message and call to action to encourage attendees to take the next step.
11. **Partner with other businesses:** Partner with complementary businesses to reach new audiences and generate leads. This could include co-hosting webinars, sharing content, or offering joint promotions.
12. **Track and analyze your results:** Use analytics to track your lead generation efforts and identify what's working and what's not. Use this information to refine your strategy and improve your results over time.

13. **Provide ongoing value:** Continue to provide value to leads even after they become customers. This could include providing educational resources, offering exclusive content, or providing excellent customer service.
14. **Use retargeting:** Use retargeting ads to reach leads who have previously engaged with your brand but haven't yet converted. This can help keep your brand top of mind and encourage them to take the next step.
15. **Segment your leads:** Segment your leads based on their interests, behavior, and demographics. This will allow you to provide more personalized and targeted communication, increasing the chances of conversion.

By combining these techniques with a strong lead nurturing process, you can build a strong pipeline of leads and increase your chances of converting them into paying customers. Remember to stay focused on providing value and building relationships with your leads, and your efforts will pay off in the long run.

**Sales presentations and proposals** are crucial elements of the sales process. They provide an opportunity to showcase your products or services and demonstrate how they can solve your prospect's pain points.

Here are some tips on how to create effective sales presentations and proposals that resonate with your target audience:

1. **Know your audience:** Before creating your sales presentation or proposal, research your audience to understand their needs, challenges, and preferences. This will help you tailor your messaging and approach to resonate with them.
2. **Focus on benefits:** Instead of just listing features, focus on the benefits of your products or services. Show how they can solve your prospect's pain points and improve their business outcomes.
3. **Keep it concise:** Your sales presentation or proposal should be clear and concise, with a logical flow. Avoid using jargon or technical terms that your audience may not understand.
4. **Use visuals:** Use visuals such as images, charts, and graphs to illustrate your points and make your presentation more engaging. This can help your audience better understand your message and retain information.
5. **Provide social proof:** Use customer testimonials, case studies, and other forms of social proof to demonstrate the value of your products or services. This can help build trust

and credibility with your audience.

6. **Address objections:** Anticipate and address potential objections that your audience may have. This can help alleviate concerns and increase the chances of conversion.
7. **Include a clear call to action:** Your sales presentation or proposal should include a clear call to action, such as scheduling a follow-up call or signing up for a free trial. This can help move your prospects further down the sales funnel.
8. **Customize your proposal:** Your proposal should be customized to the specific needs of your prospect. Use their language, address their pain points, and include relevant information to make it more compelling.
9. **Follow up:** After presenting your proposal, follow up with your prospect to answer any questions and address any concerns. This can help build trust and increase the chances of conversion.
10. **Use storytelling:** Storytelling can be a powerful way to convey your message and make an emotional connection with your audience. Use real-life examples and anecdotes to illustrate how your products or services have helped others.
11. **Show your value proposition:** Your sales presentation or proposal should clearly articulate your value proposition. Show how your products or services are unique and provide a clear advantage over your competitors.
12. **Use a structured approach:** Use a structured approach for your sales presentation or proposal, such as the problem-solution-benefit framework. This can help ensure that your messaging is clear and consistent.
13. **Tailor your presentation to the decision-maker:** If you're

presenting to a group, identify the decision-maker and tailor your presentation to their needs and preferences. This can help increase your chances of closing the deal.

14. **Use a visual hierarchy:** Use a visual hierarchy in your sales presentation or proposal to guide your audience's attention. Use larger fonts, bold text, and contrasting colors to highlight key points.
15. **Include pricing information:** Be transparent about your pricing and clearly explain the value that your products or services provide. This can help build trust and increase the likelihood of conversion.
16. **Incorporate interactivity:** Incorporate interactive elements in your sales presentation or proposal, such as quizzes or polls. This can help increase engagement and make your presentation more memorable.
17. **Use a professional design:** Use a professional design for your sales presentation or proposal. This can help convey a sense of credibility and professionalism and make your proposal more visually appealing.

**Negotiation and closing deals** are essential skills for sales managers. Here are some tactics and techniques for negotiating and closing deals effectively:

1. **Build rapport and establish trust:** Before starting negotiations, build rapport with the prospect and establish trust. Show a genuine interest in their needs and concerns.
2. **Understand the prospect's needs:** Understand the prospect's needs, goals, and pain points. This will enable you to tailor your pitch to their specific needs.
3. **Prepare thoroughly:** Prepare for negotiations by researching the prospect, their industry, and their competitors. Prepare a list of possible objections and how to overcome them.
4. **Know your value proposition:** Clearly articulate your value proposition and how it addresses the prospect's needs. Be prepared to provide evidence to support your claims.
5. **Listen actively:** Listen actively to the prospect's objections, concerns, and questions. Address them directly and honestly.
6. **Be flexible:** Be willing to compromise and find creative solutions that meet both parties' needs. Identify areas where you can offer concessions and areas where you cannot.
7. **Close the deal:** Once you have addressed all objections and concerns, close the deal by asking for the sale. Be confident, but not pushy.
8. **Follow up:** After closing the deal, follow up to ensure the

prospect is satisfied and address any issues that arise.

Here are some **additional tactics and techniques** for negotiating and closing deals:

9. **Use the power of silence:** During negotiations, use silence to your advantage. After presenting your offer, remain quiet and wait for the prospect to respond. This can be uncomfortable, but it can also prompt the prospect to make a counteroffer or accept your offer.
10. **Use social proof:** Social proof is the idea that people are more likely to believe and trust something if they see that others believe and trust it too. Use customer testimonials, case studies, and industry awards to demonstrate your product's value and build credibility.
11. **Create a sense of urgency:** Create a sense of urgency by highlighting the benefits of taking action now. For example, you could offer a limited-time discount or say that your product is in high demand and may sell out soon.
12. **Know when to walk away:** Sometimes, negotiations may reach an impasse. If you have made your best offer and the prospect is still not willing to accept it, it may be time to walk away. However, leaving the door open for future negotiations can be a good way to maintain the relationship and keep the prospect engaged.
13. **Be persistent:** Closing deals can take time, so be persistent in following up with prospects and providing them with the information they need to make a decision. However, be

respectful of their time and avoid being pushy or aggressive.

14. **Find common ground:** Look for areas of agreement and common ground with the prospect. This can help to build rapport and establish trust and can also help to identify areas where you can make concessions.
15. **Use the "anchoring" technique:** Anchoring is the idea that people tend to rely too heavily on the first piece of information they receive when making decisions. Use this to your advantage by starting negotiations with a high initial offer or price. This can make subsequent offers or prices seem more reasonable by comparison.
16. **Use the "door-in-the-face" technique:** The door-in-the-face technique involves making a large request or offer that is likely to be refused, followed by a smaller, more reasonable request, or offer. This can create a sense of reciprocity or obligation, making the prospect more likely to accept the second request or offer.
17. **Use the "foot-in-the-door" technique:** The foot-in-the-door technique involves making a small request or offer that is likely to be accepted, followed by a larger request, or offer. This can create a sense of commitment or consistency, making the prospect more likely to accept the second request or offer.
18. **Use visual aids:** Visual aids such as charts, graphs, and diagrams can be a powerful way to communicate complex information and demonstrate the benefits of your product or service. Use visual aids to support your arguments and make your pitch more compelling.
19. **Be prepared to negotiate on price:** Price is often a key consideration for prospects, so be prepared to negotiate on

price if necessary. However, be sure to emphasize the value of your product or service and avoid simply competing on price alone.

By using these negotiation tactics and techniques, you can improve your ability to close deals and achieve your sales goals. Remember to always be professional, respectful, and transparent in your negotiations, and to focus on building long-term relationships with your prospects and customers.

**Coaching and training** are essential for the ongoing success of your sales team. Here are some best practices for coaching and training your sales team to improve their performance:

1. **Set clear expectations:** Establish clear expectations for your sales team, including goals, targets, and performance metrics. This provides a clear framework for coaching and training.
2. **Provide regular feedback:** Provide regular feedback to your team members on their performance. This can help them to identify areas for improvement and make adjustments to their approach.
3. **Use data to inform coaching:** Use data and analytics to inform your coaching and training. Analyze sales performance data to identify areas of strength and weakness and use this information to tailor your coaching approach.
4. **Focus on skill development:** Focus on developing specific sales skills, such as prospecting, closing, and objection handling. Provide targeted training and coaching to help team members improve in these areas.
5. **Encourage self-reflection:** Encourage team members to reflect on their own performance and identify areas for improvement. This can help them to take ownership of their own development and improve their performance over time.
6. **Provide ongoing training:** Provide ongoing training and development opportunities for your sales team. This can include workshops, webinars, and other resources to help them stay up to date on industry trends and best practices.

7. **Lead by example:** Set a positive example for your team by demonstrating the behaviors and skills you want them to emulate. This can help to build trust and respect and can also provide a model for effective sales practices.

By using these best practices for coaching and training your sales team, you can improve their performance and drive better results for your organization. Remember to tailor your approach to the individual needs and strengths of each team member, and to provide ongoing support and encouragement as they work to improve their skills and achieve their goals.

**Sales technology and tools** have become increasingly important in today's fast-paced and competitive business environment. By using the right tools, sales teams can streamline their processes, improve their productivity, and ultimately close more deals.

Here are some of the latest sales tools and how to use them effectively:

1. **Customer Relationship Management (CRM) Software:** CRM software is a powerful tool that can help sales teams manage their customer interactions and sales pipeline. Some popular CRM software includes Salesforce, HubSpot, and Zoho. To use CRM software effectively, sales teams should ensure that all customer data is properly entered and maintained in the system, regularly review, and update their sales pipeline, and use the software to track customer interactions and follow-up tasks.
2. **Sales Engagement Platforms:** Sales engagement platforms are designed to help sales teams automate and personalize their outreach to prospects and customers. Some popular sales engagement platforms include Outreach.io, SalesLoft, and Groove. To use these tools effectively, sales teams should ensure that their messaging is personalized and relevant, use data to inform their outreach strategies and track their outreach metrics to optimize their approach over time.
3. **Sales Enablement Tools:** Sales enablement tools help sales

teams deliver the right content and messaging to prospects and customers at the right time. Some popular sales enablement tools include Highspot, Seismic, and Showpad. To use these tools effectively, sales teams should ensure that their content is up-to-date, relevant, and aligned with their sales messaging, use the tools to track content usage and effectiveness, and make adjustments to their content strategy as needed.

4. **Sales Analytics and Reporting Tools:** Sales analytics and reporting tools help sales teams track their performance and identify areas for improvement. Some popular sales analytics and reporting tools include InsightSquared, Gong, and Chorus.ai. To use these tools effectively, sales teams should regularly review their performance metrics, identify trends and patterns in their sales data, and use the insights gained to adjust their sales approach and improve their results.

5. **Sales Intelligence Tools:** Sales intelligence tools help sales teams gather insights and data on their prospects and customers, allowing them to personalize their approach and improve their sales pitch. Some popular sales intelligence tools include ZoomInfo, DiscoverOrg, and Clearbit. To use these tools effectively, sales teams should use the data to inform their outreach strategies, tailor their messaging to the specific needs of their prospects and customers, and use the insights gained to adjust their sales approach and improve their results.

6. **Sales Forecasting Tools:** Sales forecasting tools help sales teams predict future sales performance, allowing them to make informed decisions about their sales strategy and resource allocation. Some popular sales forecasting tools

include Clari, Aviso, and InsightSquared. To use these tools effectively, sales teams should regularly review their sales forecasts, adjust their approach based on their projections, and use the insights gained to optimize their sales performance.

7. **Sales Chatbots:** Sales chatbots are automated tools that can engage with prospects and customers, providing them with information and answering their questions in real time. Some popular sales chatbot tools include Drift, Intercom, and HubSpot. To use these tools effectively, sales teams should ensure that their chatbots are personalized and engaging, use them to qualify leads and gather information about prospects and customers, and integrate them with their CRM and sales engagement platforms to streamline their sales process.

8. **Video Conferencing Tools:** Video conferencing tools have become increasingly important in today's remote work environment, allowing sales teams to connect with prospects and customers from anywhere in the world. Some popular video conferencing tools include Zoom, Webex, and Microsoft Teams. To use these tools effectively, sales teams should ensure that their video conferencing technology is reliable and easy to use, use it to conduct virtual sales meetings and product demos, and integrate it with their CRM and sales engagement platforms to streamline their sales process.

9. **Sales Training and Coaching Platforms:** Sales training and coaching platforms provide sales teams with access to learning resources, coaching, and feedback to improve their sales skills. Some popular sales training and coaching platforms include SalesHood, MindTickle, and Sales

Acceleration. To use these tools effectively, sales teams should ensure that their training content is relevant and up to date, use the coaching and feedback features to improve their skills and track their progress over time.

10. **Sales Automation Tools:** Sales automation tools help sales teams automate repetitive tasks and workflows, freeing up time for more high-value activities. Some popular sales automation tools include Zapier, IFTTT, and Automate.io. To use these tools effectively, sales teams should identify the tasks and workflows that are most time-consuming or repetitive, automate those tasks using the appropriate tools, and use the time saved to focus on more strategic sales activities.
11. **Social Selling Tools:** Social selling tools help sales teams leverage social media to build relationships with prospects and customers and generate leads. Some popular social selling tools include LinkedIn Sales Navigator, Hootsuite, and Buffer. To use these tools effectively, sales teams should identify the social media platforms that are most relevant to their target audience, create compelling and engaging content, and use the tools to engage with prospects and customers in a personalized and relevant way.
12. **Sales Funnel Optimization Tools:** Sales funnel optimization tools help sales teams identify and address bottlenecks in their sales process, ultimately leading to more closed deals. Some popular sales funnel optimization tools include Crazy Egg, Hotjar, and Google Analytics. To use these tools effectively, sales teams should regularly review their sales funnel metrics, identify areas for improvement, and experiment with different strategies to optimize their sales process.

By leveraging these sales technologies and tools, sales teams can improve their productivity, streamline their processes, and ultimately close more deals. However, it's important to remember that technology is just one part of the sales equation - sales teams must also be skilled at building relationships, understanding their prospects' needs, and delivering a compelling sales pitch.

**Sales automation and CRM (Customer Relationship Management)** software can bring many benefits to your sales process by helping you manage your sales pipeline more efficiently, track customer interactions, and analyze sales data to gain insights into your business.

Here are some of the main benefits of using sales automation and CRM software:

1. **Streamlined sales process:** Sales automation software can help you automate repetitive tasks, such as data entry, lead scoring, and follow-up emails, allowing your sales reps to focus on more valuable activities, such as building relationships with customers and closing deals.
2. **Improved customer experience:** CRM software allows you to keep track of all customer interactions, including emails, phone calls, and meetings, giving you a 360-degree view of your customers. This can help you provide more personalized and relevant experiences, leading to increased customer satisfaction and loyalty.
3. **Better data analysis:** Sales automation and CRM software can help you track your sales metrics, such as conversion rates, win rates, and sales cycle length. This can help you identify areas for improvement and make data-driven decisions to optimize your sales process.
4. **Increased productivity:** By automating tasks and providing real-time data, sales automation, and CRM software can help

your sales team work more efficiently, reducing the need for manual data entry and improving collaboration across different teams.

To **implement sales automation and CRM software** effectively, here are some best practices to follow:

1. **Define your sales process:** Before implementing any software, it's important to define your sales process and identify the areas that need improvement. This can help you choose the right software that fits your needs and aligns with your business goals.
2. **Choose the right software:** There are many sales automation and CRM software options available, so it's important to choose the one that best fits your needs and budget. Consider factors such as features, ease of use, and integration with your existing tools.
3. **Train your team:** To ensure that your team can use the software effectively, provide training and support to help them learn how to use the software and understand the benefits it brings to their work.
4. **Monitor and optimize:** Once you've implemented the software, monitor its performance regularly and use data to identify areas for improvement. Continuously optimize your sales process to ensure that you're getting the most out of the software.
5. **Better sales forecasting:** By tracking your sales pipeline and analyzing historical data, sales automation, and CRM software can help you make more accurate sales forecasts, allowing you to plan and allocate resources more effectively.

6. **Improved communication:** Sales automation and CRM software can help you streamline communication across different teams, allowing for better collaboration and coordination between sales, marketing, and customer support teams.
7. **Increased customer retention:** By tracking customer interactions and gathering feedback, sales automation, and CRM software can help you identify opportunities to improve customer retention and build stronger relationships with your customers.
8. **Scalability:** As your business grows, sales automation and CRM software can help you manage your sales process more efficiently, allowing you to handle more leads and customers without sacrificing the quality of your service.
9. **Customize the software:** To get the most out of your sales automation and CRM software, customize it to fit your specific needs. This may involve configuring workflows, creating custom fields, or integrating with other tools.
10. **Focus on data quality:** To ensure that your sales data is accurate and reliable, establish data quality standards and ensure that your team adheres to them. This can help you make better decisions based on your sales data.
11. **Continuously evaluate and optimize:** The sales process is dynamic and constantly changing, so it's important to continuously evaluate and optimize your sales automation and CRM software to ensure that it's meeting your evolving business needs.

In summary, sales automation and CRM software can bring many benefits to your sales process, including improved efficiency, customer experience, data analysis, and productivity. By following best practices and customizing the software to fit your specific needs, you can implement it effectively and achieve better results for your business.

**Sales analytics and reporting** can help you gain insights into your sales process, identify areas of improvement, and make data-driven decisions to optimize your sales performance.

Here are some of the key sales analytics and reporting tools and how to use them effectively:

1. **Sales forecasting:** Sales forecasting is the process of predicting future sales based on historical data and market trends. By analyzing your sales data and market trends, you can make more accurate sales forecasts, which can help you plan and allocate resources more effectively. To use sales forecasting effectively, it's important to gather accurate sales data, establish data quality standards, and use forecasting tools or software to analyze the data and make predictions.
2. **Sales pipeline analysis:** The sales pipeline is the process that leads go through from initial contact to closing the deal. By analyzing your sales pipeline, you can identify bottlenecks and areas for improvement, such as slow-moving deals or a high number of lost deals. To analyze your sales pipeline effectively, it's important to track each stage of the pipeline and measure key metrics such as conversion rates and deal size.
3. **Lead and customer analysis:** By analyzing your leads and customers, you can gain insights into their behavior and preferences, which can help you personalize your sales and marketing efforts and improve customer retention. To analyze your leads and customers effectively, it's important

to gather data on their demographics, behavior, and interactions with your business, and use tools such as customer relationship management (CRM) software to track and analyze this data.

4. **Sales performance analysis:** Sales performance analysis involves measuring and analyzing key sales metrics, such as sales revenue, win rates, and sales cycle length. By tracking these metrics over time, you can identify trends and areas for improvement, such as a decline in win rates or an increase in the average sales cycle. To analyze sales performance effectively, it's important to establish data quality standards, track key metrics consistently, and use analytics tools or software to visualize and analyze the data.
5. **Sales team performance analysis:** Sales team performance analysis involves measuring and analyzing the performance of your sales team, such as individual sales rep performance, team productivity, and training needs. By analyzing your sales team's performance, you can identify areas for improvement and provide targeted coaching and training to help them improve. To analyze sales team performance effectively, it's important to establish performance metrics and goals, track individual and team performance consistently, and use analytics and reporting tools to visualize and analyze the data.

In summary, sales analytics and reporting can help you gain valuable insights into your sales process, identify areas for improvement, and make data-driven decisions to optimize your sales performance. By tracking key metrics and using analytics and reporting tools effectively, you can gain a competitive edge and grow your business.

**Sales and marketing alignment** is critical for achieving your business objectives because it helps to ensure that your teams are working towards the same goals. When sales and marketing teams are aligned, they can work together to create a consistent message and customer experience, leading to increased revenue and customer satisfaction.

Here are some ways to align your sales and marketing teams for maximum impact:

1. **Establish shared goals:** Set clear, shared goals for both teams that align with your overall business objectives. This will help to ensure that everyone is working towards the same outcomes.
2. **Foster open communication:** Encourage open communication between sales and marketing teams. This can include regular meetings, joint planning sessions, and shared data and insights.
3. **Develop a shared understanding of the customer:** Sales and marketing teams should have a shared understanding of your target customers. This can include their pain points, motivations, and purchasing behaviors.
4. **Create a shared language:** Sales and marketing teams should use a shared language to describe your products and services. This can help to avoid confusion and ensure that everyone is speaking the same language when communicating with customers.

5. **Measure and analyze results:** Regularly measure and analyze the results of your sales and marketing efforts. This can help to identify areas for improvement and ensure that both teams are working effectively towards your shared goals.
6. **Develop buyer personas:** Create detailed buyer personas that outline the characteristics, needs, and behaviors of your ideal customers. This will help both teams to tailor their messaging and approach to better resonate with your target audience.
7. **Share content and collateral:** Provide sales teams with marketing collateral, such as case studies, whitepapers, and presentations, that they can use to support their sales efforts. This ensures that they have the most up-to-date and relevant information to share with customers.
8. **Use shared technology:** Implement shared technology, such as a customer relationship management (CRM) system, that both sales and marketing teams can use to track customer interactions and measure results. This can help to improve collaboration and streamline processes between the two teams.
9. **Encourage cross-functional training:** Provide opportunities for sales and marketing teams to learn from each other and gain a deeper understanding of each other's roles and responsibilities. This can help to foster a culture of collaboration and alignment.
10. **Celebrate shared successes:** Celebrate successes that are achieved through collaboration between sales and marketing teams. This can help to reinforce the importance of alignment and encourage continued collaboration in the future.

11. **Define the lead handoff process:** Establish a clear handoff process for leads between sales and marketing teams. This involves defining the criteria for when a lead is ready to be handed off from marketing to sales and ensuring that the handoff process is seamless and efficient.
12. **Develop a content strategy:** Develop a content strategy that aligns with your sales goals and target audience. This will ensure that marketing creates content that is relevant and useful for the sales team to use in their conversations with prospects and customers.
13. **Hold joint planning sessions:** Hold regular joint planning sessions between sales and marketing teams to ensure that both teams are aligned on the overall strategy, goals, and tactics. These sessions can help to identify new opportunities for collaboration and ensure that both teams are working towards the same objectives.
14. **Foster a culture of collaboration:** Encourage collaboration between sales and marketing teams by recognizing and rewarding cross-functional efforts and successes. This can help to create a culture of collaboration and alignment that extends beyond just these two teams.
15. **Continuously measure and optimize:** Continuously measure and optimize your sales and marketing efforts. This involves analyzing data and adjusting strategies to improve performance and ensure that both teams are working towards the same goals.

By implementing these tips, you can help to ensure that your sales and marketing teams are aligned and working together to achieve your business objectives. This alignment can result in improved customer experiences, increased revenue, and greater efficiency and effectiveness across your organization.

**Building and maintaining strong customer relationships** is crucial for the long-term success of any business. Here are some techniques that can help:

1. **Listen to your customers:** Listen to what your customers have to say and pay attention to their needs, wants, and concerns. This will help you to better understand their perspective and tailor your approach to meet their needs.
2. **Be responsive:** Respond to your customers in a timely and helpful manner. Whether it's a question, concern, or feedback, make sure to acknowledge and address it promptly.
3. **Personalize your approach:** Personalize your interactions with your customers by using their names and remembering details about their preferences and past interactions. This helps to build a strong rapport and make them feel valued.
4. **Go above and beyond:** Surprise and delight your customers by going above and beyond their expectations. This might include offering discounts or bonuses, providing exceptional customer service, or simply taking the time to follow up and check in on their satisfaction.
5. **Offer loyalty programs:** Offer loyalty programs to incentivize repeat business and reward customers for their loyalty. This can include discounts, exclusive offers, or other perks that make them feel valued and appreciated.
6. **Continuously improve:** Continuously seek feedback from your customers and use it to improve your products, services, and overall customer experience. This shows that

you value their opinion and are committed to delivering the best possible experience.

7. **Be transparent:** Be transparent with your customers about your business practices and policies. This helps to build trust and establish a sense of honesty and integrity.
8. **Offer exceptional customer service:** Provide exceptional customer service by being friendly, helpful, and knowledgeable. Respond to inquiries promptly and handle any issues or concerns with empathy and understanding.
9. **Maintain consistent communication:** Keep your customers informed about important updates, changes, or promotions through regular communication channels such as email, social media, or newsletters.
10. **Build a community:** Build a community around your brand by creating a forum or social media group where customers can interact with each other and share their experiences.
11. **Show appreciation:** Show your customers that you appreciate their business by sending thank you notes, offering special discounts or promotions, or recognizing their loyalty through a rewards program.
12. **Be adaptable:** Be adaptable and willing to change your approach based on feedback and changing customer needs. This shows that you are responsive to their needs and committed to providing the best possible experience.
13. **Provide value:** Provide value to your customers beyond just your products or services. This can include providing educational resources, offering personalized recommendations, or sharing industry insights and trends.
14. **Foster a positive company culture:** Foster a positive

company culture that values customer satisfaction and encourages employees to go above and beyond to meet customer needs. Happy employees are more likely to provide exceptional service and create a positive experience for your customers.

15. **Use customer feedback to inform business decisions:** Use customer feedback to inform business decisions and improve your products, services, and overall customer experience. This shows that you value their opinion and are committed to providing the best possible experience.
16. **Be consistent:** Be consistent in your approach to customer service and communication. This helps to establish trust and reliability and ensures that customers know what to expect every time they interact with your business.
17. **Be authentic:** Be genuine and authentic in your interactions with customers. This helps to build trust and establish a sense of authenticity and credibility.
18. **Build partnerships:** Build partnerships with other businesses or organizations that share your values and can help to enhance your customer experience. This can help to expand your reach and provide additional value to your customers.

By implementing these techniques, you can build and maintain strong customer relationships that will help your business thrive in the long run. Remember, building and maintaining strong customer relationships is an ongoing process that requires dedication and a customer- centric mindset. By prioritizing your customers and continuously seeking ways to improve their experience, you can set your business up for long-term success.

**Account management** is indeed a critical function of a sales manager, especially when it comes to managing key accounts. Here are some best practices for account management and building strong relationships with your most important customers:

1. **Develop a deep understanding of your customer's business:** To effectively manage a key account, it's important to have a thorough understanding of their business objectives, challenges, and pain points. This will enable you to provide personalized solutions that meet their specific needs.
2. **Build strong relationships with key decision-makers:** Identify the key decision-makers within your customer's organization and build strong relationships with them. This will help you understand their priorities and influence their decisions.
3. **Communicate regularly:** Keep your key accounts informed about new products, services, and promotions. Regular communication helps build trust and strengthens the relationship.
4. **Provide exceptional service:** Ensure that your customer is satisfied with the products and services they receive. Address any issues promptly and go above and beyond to exceed their expectations.
5. **Be proactive:** Anticipate your customer's needs and offer solutions before they even ask for them. This proactive approach demonstrates your commitment to their success and strengthens the relationship.

6. **Collaborate on strategic initiatives:** Work closely with your key accounts to identify opportunities for growth and collaborate on strategic initiatives. This partnership approach can lead to mutually beneficial outcomes.
7. **Measure and track performance:** Establish key performance indicators (KPIs) and regularly track progress against them. This will help you identify areas for improvement and demonstrate the value you bring to your customer.
8. **Provide thought leadership:** Share insights and best practices with your key accounts. This can include research reports, case studies, and industry trends. By providing value beyond just your products or services, you can position yourself as a trusted advisor.
9. **Be flexible and adaptable:** Key accounts often have unique requirements and preferences. Be flexible and adaptable to meet their needs, even if it means deviating from your standard processes or procedures.
10. **Understand the competition:** Be aware of your customer's competitive landscape and how your products or services compare. This will enable you to position yourself as a strategic partner and offer insights and solutions that help your customer stay ahead of the competition.
11. **Foster a culture of collaboration:** Encourage collaboration between your sales, marketing, and customer service teams to ensure a seamless customer experience. This can include sharing customer feedback, coordinating promotions, and jointly developing solutions.
12. **Continuously improve:** Solicit feedback from your key accounts and use it to continuously improve your products,

services, and processes. This demonstrates your commitment to their success and helps build trust and loyalty.

13. **Invest in training:** Ensure that your sales team is well-trained in your products, services, and processes. This will enable them to provide knowledgeable and professional service to your key accounts.
14. **Create a customized account plan:** Develop a customized account plan for each key account that outlines their specific goals, challenges, and opportunities. This will enable you to tailor your approach and solutions to their unique needs.
15. **Set clear expectations:** Be clear about what your key accounts can expect from you in terms of service, support, and communication. This will help manage their expectations and ensure a positive customer experience.
16. **Celebrate successes:** Celebrate your key accounts' successes and milestones. This demonstrates your commitment to their success and strengthens the relationship.
17. **Be transparent:** Be transparent about your pricing, policies, and processes. This builds trust and helps avoid misunderstandings that can strain the relationship.
18. **Provide excellent post-sales support:** Ensure that your key accounts receive excellent post-sales support. This includes timely and effective problem resolution, as well as ongoing training and education.

By incorporating these best practices into your account management strategy, you can build strong relationships with your key accounts and position your business for long-term success.

**Sales territory management** is a critical aspect of sales strategy that involves dividing a sales force into regions or territories to maximize revenue and productivity. Effective sales territory management can help organizations ensure that their sales efforts are targeted toward the right customers and prospects, leading to increased sales and revenue growth.

Here are some strategies to manage sales territories effectively:

1. **Define your territories:** Start by defining your sales territories based on factors such as geography, customer demographics, sales potential, and competition. This will help you create a clear and structured sales plan for each territory.
2. **Allocate resources wisely:** Allocate sales resources based on the sales potential of each territory. Give priority to high-potential territories and allocate more resources to them while ensuring that low-potential territories receive adequate attention.
3. **Set goals and objectives:** Set clear and measurable goals and objectives for each sales territory. This will help your sales team stay focused and motivated and will also provide a basis for measuring performance.
4. **Provide training and support:** Provide your sales team with the right training, tools, and support to help them succeed in their territories. This could include training on product knowledge, sales techniques, and customer relationship

management.

5. **Monitor and evaluate performance:** Regularly monitor and evaluate the performance of your sales team in each territory. Use this data to identify areas for improvement and to adjust your sales strategy as needed.
6. **Collaborate and share best practices:** Encourage collaboration and information sharing among your sales team members. This can help them learn from each other, share best practices, and identify new sales opportunities.
7. **Use data and analytics:** Use data and analytics to gain insights into customer behavior, sales trends, and market conditions in each territory. This can help you identify new sales opportunities, adjust your sales strategy, and make data-driven decisions.
8. **Segment your customers:** Segment your customers based on factors such as industry, company size, and buying behavior. This will help you tailor your sales approach to each customer segment and maximize your chances of success.
9. **Develop a territory plan:** Develop a detailed territory plan for each sales territory, including a list of target accounts, key contacts, and sales objectives. This plan should be reviewed and updated regularly to reflect changes in the market and customer needs.
10. **Foster a culture of accountability:** Foster a culture of accountability by setting clear expectations for your sales team and holding them accountable for achieving their sales goals. This can help create a sense of ownership and motivation among your sales team members.
11. **Provide incentives and rewards:** Provide incentives and

rewards to motivate your sales team and recognize their achievements. This could include bonuses, commissions, and other performance-based rewards.

12. **Continuously improve:** Continuously improve your sales territory management strategy by soliciting feedback from your sales team and customers, and by staying up to date with industry trends and best practices.
13. **Foster collaboration with other departments:** Encourage collaboration between your sales team and other departments such as marketing and customer service. This can help ensure a coordinated approach to customer engagement and maximize the impact of your sales efforts.
14. **Utilize technology:** Use technology to streamline your sales processes and improve communication and collaboration among your sales team. This could include using CRM systems, sales automation tools, and mobile applications to help your sales team stay productive and efficient.
15. **Provide ongoing training and development:** Provide ongoing training and development opportunities to help your sales team stay up to date with the latest sales techniques, product knowledge, and industry trends. This can help them identify new sales opportunities and better serve their customers.
16. **Measure and track performance:** Use key performance indicators (KPIs) to measure and track the performance of your sales team in each territory. This can help you identify areas for improvement, adjust your sales strategy, and recognize high-performing sales reps.
17. **Establish a sales culture:** Establish a sales culture that encourages innovation, collaboration, and continuous

improvement. This can help create a positive and productive work environment that motivates your sales team to achieve their goals.

18. **Continuously evaluate and refine your strategy:** Continuously evaluate and refine your sales territory management strategy based on feedback from your sales team, customers, and market conditions. This can help ensure that your approach remains effective and relevant over time.

In summary, effective sales territory management requires a combination of strategic planning, data analysis, collaboration, technology, training, and performance management. By implementing these strategies and continuously refining your approach, you can optimize your sales efforts in each region and drive revenue growth for your organization.

**Sales incentives and compensation** can indeed be powerful motivators for your sales team. When designed effectively, they can drive results and lead to increased sales and revenue for your business.

Here are some best practices for designing incentive programs and compensation plans that can help you achieve your sales goals:

1. **Set Clear and Measurable Sales Goals:** The first step in designing a successful incentive program is to set clear and measurable sales goals. These goals should be aligned with your overall business objectives and tied to specific metrics such as revenue, units sold, or customer acquisition. Make sure that your sales team understands the goals and knows what they need to do to achieve them.
2. **Use a Mix of Incentives:** A successful incentive program should use a mix of incentives to motivate your sales team. This can include bonuses, commissions, and non-monetary rewards such as recognition or career advancement opportunities. Using a mix of incentives can help keep your sales team engaged and motivated over the long term.
3. **Make Incentives Attainable:** Incentives should be challenging but attainable. If incentives are too difficult to achieve, your sales team may become demotivated and disengaged. On the other hand, if incentives are too easy to achieve, they may not provide enough motivation to drive sales.

4. **Use Performance Data to Determine Compensation:** When designing a compensation plan, use performance data to determine how much each sales team member should be paid. This can include metrics such as revenue generated, units sold, or customer satisfaction ratings. By using performance data to determine compensation, you can ensure that top performers are rewarded for their efforts.
5. **Communicate Clearly and Often:** Communication is key when it comes to designing an effective incentive program. Make sure that your sales team understands the program and how it works. Provide regular updates on performance and progress toward goals. Celebrate successes and recognize top performers to keep your team engaged and motivated.
6. **Consider the Sales Cycle:** When designing an incentive program, consider the length of your sales cycle. If it takes a long time to close deals, consider using incentives that reward progress toward goals rather than just final outcomes. For example, you could offer bonuses for setting up initial meetings or reaching certain milestones in the sales process.
7. **Align Incentives with Customer Needs:** Your incentive program should be designed to align with the needs of your customers. For example, if your customers value customer service, consider using incentives that reward your sales team for providing excellent customer service.
8. **Provide Training and Support:** Incentive programs are most effective when your sales team has the skills and knowledge they need to succeed. Provide training and support to help your team develop the skills they need to achieve their goals.
9. **Evaluate and Adjust:** Finally, it's important to regularly

evaluate your incentive program and compensation plan to ensure that they are working effectively. Use performance data to identify areas of improvement and make adjustments as needed.

10. **Consider Team Goals:** While individual incentives are important, it's also important to consider team goals. Consider using incentives that reward the team as a whole for achieving certain milestones or targets. This can help foster a sense of collaboration and teamwork among your sales team.
11. **Keep it Simple:** Incentive programs and compensation plans should be simple and easy to understand. Avoid using complex formulas or metrics that are difficult to calculate. Instead, use straightforward metrics that are easy to track and understand.
12. **Balance Short-term and Long-term Goals:** While it's important to focus on short-term goals, it's also important to consider long-term goals. Consider using a mix of short-term and long-term incentives to motivate your sales team to achieve both immediate and long-term objectives.
13. **Be Transparent:** Transparency is key when it comes to designing an effective incentive program. Make sure that your sales team understands how incentives are calculated and how they can earn rewards. This can help build trust and ensure that your sales team is fully engaged in the program.
14. **Reward for Quality, Not Just Quantity:** While it's important to reward your sales team for achieving sales targets, it's also important to consider the quality of their work. Consider using incentives that reward your sales team for providing excellent customer service, building strong

relationships, or achieving other qualitative goals.

By following these additional best practices, you can design an incentive program and compensation plan that motivates your sales team to achieve their goals, fosters collaboration and teamwork, and drives results for your business.

**Sales forecasting and pipeline analysis** are essential tools for any company looking to improve its sales process and drive growth.

Here are some best practices for effective forecasting and pipeline analysis:

1. **Define the stages of your sales:** To accurately track your pipeline, you need to define your sales stages. This allows you to measure progress and identify where deals may be getting stuck. Your sales stages should reflect the key milestones in your sales process, such as initial contact, discovery, proposal, negotiation, and closing.
2. **Use data to inform your forecasts:** Accurate sales forecasts require data-driven analysis. You need to track historical sales data, win rates, conversion rates, and deal sizes to accurately predict future sales. Use your CRM system to gather this data and create reports that can help you forecast future sales.
3. **Regularly review and update your pipeline:** Your sales pipeline is constantly changing, so it's important to regularly review and update it. This allows you to identify potential issues before they become problems and adjust your sales strategy accordingly. Use your CRM system to track progress and update the status of each deal in your pipeline.
4. **Analyze your pipeline for potential issues:** Use your pipeline analysis to identify potential issues that may be preventing you from closing deals. Look for deals that have been stuck in a particular stage for an extended period, deals

with low win rates, and deals with low deal sizes. This information can help you adjust your sales process to improve your chances of closing deals.

5. **Use your forecasting and pipeline analysis to inform your sales strategy:** Use the insights you gain from your forecasting and pipeline analysis to inform your sales strategy. For example, if you notice that deals are getting stuck in the negotiation stage, you may need to adjust your pricing or offer more flexible payment terms. Or, if you notice that your win rates are low in a particular market segment, you may need to adjust your messaging or target a different segment.
6. **Involve your sales team in the process:** Your sales team is on the front lines of your sales process, so it's important to involve them in the forecasting and pipeline analysis process. They can provide valuable insights into the status of each deal and potential roadblocks that may be preventing them from closing deals. This collaboration can help you identify issues and adjust your sales strategy more effectively.
7. **Use multiple forecasting methodologies:** There are several different methodologies you can use for sales forecasting, including historical analysis, opportunity stage forecasting, and pipeline analysis. It's a good idea to use multiple methodologies to create a more accurate forecast. For example, you can use historical analysis to predict overall sales growth and opportunity stage forecasting to predict the likelihood of closing individual deals.
8. **Regularly communicate with stakeholders:** Keep your stakeholders informed of your sales forecasting and pipeline analysis results. This includes your sales team, executives,

and investors. Regular communication can help build trust and alignment around your sales strategy.

9. **Set realistic targets:** When creating your sales forecast, it's important to set realistic targets that are achievable based on your historical data and market conditions. Unrealistic targets can lead to sales team burnout and demotivation.
10. **Continuously monitor and adjust your sales process:** Your sales process is not static, and it's important to continuously monitor and adjust it to improve your chances of closing deals. Use your pipeline analysis to identify areas in your sales process that need improvement and adjust your strategy accordingly.
11. **Use a CRM system:** A customer relationship management (CRM) system can help you track your sales pipeline, analyze data, and generate reports. It's a valuable tool for managing your sales process and forecasting future sales.
12. **Track leading indicators:** Leading indicators are metrics that can help you predict future sales, such as the number of new leads generated, or the number of proposals sent out. Tracking leading indicators can help you adjust your sales strategy in real time and improve your chances of closing deals.
13. **Use scenario planning:** Scenario planning involves creating multiple sales forecasts based on different scenarios, such as changes in market conditions or sales team performance. This can help you prepare for different outcomes and adjust your sales strategy accordingly.
14. **Focus on quality over quantity:** It's important to focus on the quality of your sales pipeline rather than the quantity. A smaller pipeline with higher-quality leads is more likely to

result in closed deals than a larger pipeline with low-quality leads.

15. **Regularly review your sales goals:** It's important to regularly review your sales goals and adjust them as needed. This can help keep your sales team motivated and aligned with your overall sales strategy.

By following these additional tips, you can create a more effective sales forecasting and pipeline analysis process to drive growth and improve your sales process.

**Sales training and development** are critical components of any successful sales team. With the constantly evolving sales landscape, it is essential to keep your team up to date on the latest techniques and strategies to ensure that they are equipped to meet the changing needs of your customers.

Here are some best practices for sales training and development:

1. **Develop a comprehensive training program:** A well-designed training program should cover all aspects of sales, from prospecting to closing deals. The program should be tailored to the specific needs of your team and should include both classroom and hands-on training.
2. **Use a variety of training methods:** People learn in different ways, so it is essential to use a variety of training methods, including videos, role-playing, case studies, and online courses, to provide a well-rounded learning experience.
3. **Provide ongoing training:** Sales training should not be a one-time event. To keep your team up to date on the latest techniques and strategies, provide ongoing training and development opportunities.
4. **Encourage continuous learning:** Create a culture of continuous learning by encouraging your team to read sales books and attend industry events. Provide opportunities for them to share what they have learned with the rest of the team.
5. **Measure the effectiveness of your training:** Track the

performance of your team before and after training to measure the effectiveness of your training program. Use this data to make adjustments to your program as needed.

6. **Focus on skills development:** When designing your training program, focus on developing the specific skills that your team needs to succeed in their roles. This may include communication skills, negotiation skills, or product knowledge.
7. **Incorporate real-world scenarios:** To make your training program more engaging and effective, incorporate real-world scenarios that your team is likely to encounter in their day-to-day work. This will help them apply their training to real-life situations.
8. **Offer coaching and feedback:** In addition to formal training sessions, offer one-on-one coaching and feedback sessions to help your team members improve their skills. This can be particularly effective for addressing specific areas where an individual may be struggling.
9. **Use technology to your advantage:** There are many tools and technologies available that can enhance your sales training program. Consider using video conferencing, online learning platforms, or mobile apps to provide your team with flexible and convenient training options.
10. **Make training a priority:** Finally, it is essential to make training and development a priority for your team. This means setting aside dedicated time and resources for training and communicating the importance of ongoing learning to your team members.
11. **Lead by example:** As a leader, it's important to model the behavior that you want to see in your team. Make sure that

you are also continuously learning and seeking out new knowledge and skills.

12. **Encourage collaboration:** Encourage your team members to collaborate and share ideas with each other. This can be done through regular team meetings, brainstorming sessions, or even online forums or chat groups.
13. **Provide opportunities for growth:** Provide your team members with opportunities for growth and advancement within the organization. This could include promotions, leadership development programs, or cross-functional training.
14. **Celebrate successes:** Celebrate the successes of your team members and recognize their accomplishments. This can help to create a positive and supportive team culture that encourages ongoing learning and development.
15. **Solicit feedback:** Finally, it's important to regularly solicit feedback from your team members regarding their training and development needs. This can help you to tailor your training program to the specific needs of your team and ensure that they are getting the support they need to succeed.

By implementing these strategies, you can create a culture of continuous learning within your sales team that will help them stay up to date on the latest techniques and strategies, and ultimately drive success for your organization.

**Optimizing your sales process** is crucial for achieving consistent sales success and growth. Here are some best practices for optimizing your sales process:

1. **Define your sales process:** Define each step of your sales process and create a detailed roadmap for your sales team to follow. This will help your team stay focused and ensure that each lead is being handled consistently.
2. **Identify your ideal customer profile:** Identify the characteristics of your ideal customer and tailor your messaging and sales approach to their needs and preferences.
3. **Qualify leads effectively:** Develop a clear set of criteria for qualifying leads and ensure that your sales team is following this process consistently. This will help your team focus their efforts on leads that are most likely to convert into customers.
4. **Utilize technology:** Use technology to automate repetitive tasks and streamline your sales process. This can include tools for lead scoring, email automation, and customer relationship management (CRM) software.
5. **Measure and analyze:** Regularly track and analyze key metrics such as conversion rates, average deal size, and sales cycle length. Use this data to identify areas of improvement and adjust your sales process accordingly.
6. **Align sales and marketing:** Ensure that your sales and marketing teams are aligned and working together towards a common goal. This can include developing a shared

understanding of your target audience and creating consistent messaging across all touchpoints.

7. **Focus on building relationships:** Building strong relationships with your prospects and customers is key to achieving long-term success. Encourage your sales team to focus on building trust and credibility with their prospects, rather than just trying to close a deal.
8. **Provide ongoing training and support:** Salespeople need ongoing training and support to stay motivated and perform at their best. This can include regular coaching sessions, training workshops, and access to resources such as sales playbooks and competitive intelligence.
9. **Continually test and optimize:** Your sales process should be constantly evolving and improving based on feedback and data. Encourage your team to experiment with new techniques and approaches, and regularly test and analyze the results.
10. **Maintain a customer-centric focus:** Your sales process should always be focused on meeting the needs and preferences of your customers. Make sure your team is listening to customer feedback and adjusting their approach accordingly.
11. **Develop a sales playbook:** A sales playbook is a valuable resource for your sales team, providing a detailed guide to your sales process, best practices, and key messaging. Use your sales playbook to ensure that your team is consistently following your sales process and delivering a consistent message to prospects.
12. **Use data to inform your decisions:** Data can provide valuable insights into the effectiveness of your sales process.

Use data to identify trends, track performance, and identify areas for improvement.

13. **Leverage social proof:** Social proof, such as customer testimonials and case studies, can be a powerful tool for building credibility and trust with prospects. Incorporate social proof into your sales process to help overcome objections and close deals.
14. **Personalize your approach:** Personalization is key to building strong relationships with prospects and customers. Use data and insights to tailor your messaging and approach to each individual prospect.
15. **Foster a culture of learning:** Encourage your sales team to learn from each other and share best practices. Foster a culture of continuous learning and improvement to keep your team motivated and engaged.

By implementing these additional tips, you can further optimize your sales process and improve your chances of success. Remember, optimizing your sales process is an ongoing effort that requires continuous attention and refinement. By staying focused on your customers' needs and preferences and continually testing and refining your approach, you can achieve long-term sales success.

**Sales and Operational Planning** (S&OP) is a critical process for any business that wants to align its sales and operational efforts and achieve better business outcomes. S&OP is a collaborative process that involves various departments within an organization, including sales, marketing, finance, production, and supply chain.

The following are some best practices for effective Sales and Operational Planning:

1. **Establish a cross-functional team:** A cross-functional team should be established to ensure that all departments are involved in the planning process. This team should be led by a senior executive who can make decisions and ensure that the process is followed.
2. **Develop a rolling forecast:** A rolling forecast should be developed with the ability to update it regularly. This will help to ensure that the plan remains relevant and responsive to changes in the market, customer demand, and other factors.
3. **Use data to drive decision-making:** Data should be used to inform decision-making. This means that all departments should provide accurate and timely data to the S&OP team, which can then use this data to make informed decisions.
4. **Ensure that the plan is flexible:** The plan should be flexible enough to accommodate changes in the market, customer demand, and other factors. This may require changes to the production schedule, inventory levels, and other operational

aspects.

5. **Communicate the plan effectively:** The plan should be communicated effectively to all departments within the organization. This will help to ensure that everyone understands what is expected of them and can work towards achieving the same goals.
6. **Involve key stakeholders:** It's important to involve key stakeholders in the S&OP process, including customers, suppliers, and distributors. This can help ensure that their needs are taken into account and that the plan is aligned with their requirements.
7. **Establish performance metrics:** Performance metrics should be established to track progress and measure success. These metrics should be aligned with the overall business objectives and should be regularly reviewed and updated.
8. **Conduct scenario planning:** Scenario planning involves creating "what-if" scenarios to anticipate potential changes in the market, customer demand, or other factors. This can help businesses to be better prepared for unexpected events and to respond quickly to changing conditions.
9. **Regularly review and update the plan:** The S&OP plan should be reviewed and updated regularly to ensure that it remains relevant and effective. This may require adjustments to the production schedule, inventory levels, and other operational aspects.
10. **Use technology to support the process:** Technology can be used to support the S&OP process, including forecasting tools, demand planning software, and supply chain management systems. These tools can help businesses to automate processes, improve accuracy, and reduce the time

required to complete the planning process.

11. **Emphasize collaboration:** Collaboration is key to successful S&OP. Encourage open communication and collaboration between departments to ensure that everyone is working towards the same goals.
12. **Ensure buy-in from all stakeholders:** All stakeholders involved in the S&OP process should be fully committed to the plan. This includes senior executives, department heads, and frontline staff. Make sure everyone understands the importance of the plan and their role in its success.
13. **Balance supply and demand:** A key objective of S&OP is to balance supply and demand. This can help to avoid overproduction or stockouts, which can negatively impact customer satisfaction and profitability.
14. **Consider multiple time horizons:** S&OP should consider multiple time horizons, including short-term, medium-term, and long-term planning. This can help to ensure that the plan is aligned with the overall business strategy and that the organization is prepared for future changes in the market.
15. **Monitor and measure performance:** Regularly monitor and measure performance against established metrics. This can help to identify areas for improvement and ensure that the plan is delivering the desired results.
16. **Continuously improve the process:** S&OP is an ongoing process that should be continuously improved. Solicit feedback from stakeholders and make adjustments to the process as needed to ensure that it remains effective.

By following these additional tips, businesses can ensure that their Sales and Operational Planning process is effective and delivers the desired outcomes. S&OP is a complex and ongoing process, but with the right approach and commitment, it can help businesses to achieve their goals and succeed in today's competitive marketplace.

**Integrating your sales and customer service efforts** is a smart business move that can help you provide a seamless and cohesive customer experience.

Here are some strategies for integrating your sales and customer service departments:

1. **Encourage Collaboration:** Encourage collaboration between your sales and customer service teams. Encourage them to share information and insights about customers, leads, and prospects. This can help your teams better understand customer needs and preferences, which can help them create more effective sales and customer service strategies.
2. **Leverage Technology:** Use technology to integrate your sales and customer service efforts. For instance, you can use customer relationship management (CRM) software to track customer interactions across different channels. This can help your teams provide more personalized and timely support to customers.
3. **Foster a Customer-Centric Culture:** Foster a customer-centric culture in your organization. Encourage your teams to put the needs and preferences of customers first. This can help your sales and customer service teams work together more effectively to create a seamless customer experience.
4. **Provide Training:** Provide training to your sales and customer service teams. This can help them develop the

skills and knowledge they need to work together more effectively. For instance, you can provide customer service training to your sales reps, or sales training to your customer service reps.

5. **Measure and Optimize:** Measure the impact of your sales and customer service integration efforts. Use data to identify areas for improvement and optimize your strategies for maximum impact. For instance, you can track customer satisfaction metrics, sales conversion rates, and customer retention rates to gauge the effectiveness of your integration efforts.
6. **Align Goals and Metrics:** Align the goals and metrics of your sales and customer service teams. This can help ensure that both teams are working towards the same objectives and that their efforts are mutually reinforcing. For instance, you can set common goals for sales revenue and customer satisfaction, and track metrics such as response times and resolution rates across both teams.
7. **Use Feedback Loops:** Use feedback loops to ensure that customer feedback is shared between your sales and customer service teams. For instance, you can use customer feedback surveys to gather insights on customer needs and preferences and share this information with your sales team to help them tailor their sales pitches and messaging.
8. **Develop a Single View of the Customer:** Develop a single view of the customer across your sales and customer service departments. This can help your teams better understand customer behavior and preferences and provide more personalized and relevant support. For instance, you can use customer data analytics to analyze customer interactions

across different channels and create a unified customer profile that can be accessed by both teams.

9. **Streamline Processes:** Streamline your sales and customer service processes to ensure that they are aligned and integrated. For instance, you can create a common process for handling customer inquiries and complaints and ensure that both teams have access to the same customer information and support tools.
10. **Foster a Continuous Improvement Culture:** Foster a culture of continuous improvement in your sales and customer service teams. Encourage them to share ideas and feedback on how to improve the customer experience and use this feedback to refine your integration strategies over time.
11. **Empower Your Teams:** Empower your sales and customer service teams to make decisions and take actions that are in the best interest of the customer. This can help them provide more personalized and responsive support to customers and improve the overall customer experience.
12. **Use Social Media:** Use social media to integrate your sales and customer service efforts. For instance, you can use social media platforms to engage with customers, respond to inquiries and complaints, and promote your products and services. This can help you build a strong online presence and create a more seamless customer experience across different channels.
13. **Create a Knowledge Base:** Create a knowledge base that can be accessed by both your sales and customer service teams. This can help your teams quickly find answers to common customer questions and provide more consistent and

accurate support. You can also use your knowledge base to capture customer insights, feedback, and preferences, which can help you refine your sales and customer service strategies over time.

14. **Foster a Culture of Communication:** Foster a culture of open communication between your sales and customer service teams. Encourage them to share information and insights on customer needs and preferences, and work together to create more effective sales and customer service strategies. This can help you identify new opportunities for growth and improve the overall customer experience.
15. **Monitor and Measure Performance:** Monitor and measure the performance of your sales and customer service teams. Use data analytics to track key metrics such as customer satisfaction, sales conversion rates, and customer retention rates. This can help you identify areas for improvement and optimize your integration strategies for maximum impact.

By implementing these strategies, you can create a truly integrated sales and customer service experience that can help you build strong customer relationships, increase customer loyalty, and drive business growth.

**Collaboration between sales and product development teams** is important because it helps ensure that products are developed with the customer's needs in mind.

Here are some best practices for collaboration between these two teams:

1. **Foster open communication:** Encourage regular communication between sales and product development teams. Create channels for communication such as regular meetings, email, and collaboration tools like Slack or Microsoft Teams. This will help ensure that both teams are on the same page regarding customer needs, product features, and timelines.
2. **Involve sales in product development:** Involve sales representatives in the product development process. Sales representatives can provide valuable insights into customer needs, pain points, and preferences. This can help ensure that products are developed with the customer in mind.
3. **Share customer feedback:** Sales representatives are often the first point of contact for customers. Encourage sales representatives to share customer feedback with the product development team. This feedback can help inform product development decisions and ensure that products meet customer needs.
4. **Set shared goals:** Establish shared goals for both sales and product development teams. This will help ensure that both

teams are working toward the same objectives and will help create a culture of collaboration and teamwork.

5. **Celebrate successes:** Celebrate successes and milestones achieved by both sales and product development teams. This will help foster a culture of innovation and encourage both teams to continue working together.

To create a **culture of innovation**, you can:

1. **Encourage experimentation:** Encourage both sales and product development teams to experiment with new ideas and approaches. This can help foster a culture of innovation and creativity.
2. **Embrace failure:** Encourage both teams to embrace failure as a learning opportunity. This can help reduce the fear of failure and encourage experimentation and risk-taking.
3. **Provide training and development opportunities:** Provide training and development opportunities for both sales and product development teams. This can help them develop new skills and knowledge and stay up to date with the latest trends and technologies.
4. **Recognize and reward innovation:** Recognize and reward individuals or teams who come up with innovative ideas or approaches. This can help foster a culture of innovation and encourage both teams to continue working together to develop new and innovative products.
5. **Encourage cross-functional collaboration:** Encourage collaboration between teams across different departments and functions. This can help break down silos and encourage the sharing of ideas and expertise.
6. **Create a safe space for ideas:** Create a safe space for individuals to share their ideas and opinions without fear of judgment or criticism. Encourage open and respectful communication and create a culture where everyone's ideas

are valued.

7. **Provide resources and support:** Provide the necessary resources, tools, and support for individuals and teams to pursue innovative ideas and projects. This can include access to funding, time, and expertise.
8. **Foster a growth mindset:** Encourage a growth mindset, where individuals and teams are encouraged to learn from failures and mistakes and continue to improve and innovate.
9. **Lead by example:** Leaders play a critical role in shaping organizational culture. Encourage leaders to lead by example and demonstrate a commitment to innovation and collaboration.
10. **Measure and track progress:** Set goals and measures of success for innovation initiatives. Regularly track progress and celebrate successes. This can help build momentum and encourage continued innovation and collaboration.
11. **Encourage diversity and inclusivity:** Encourage diversity of thought and perspectives by building a diverse team. This can help foster a culture of innovation by bringing together individuals with different experiences, backgrounds, and ideas.
12. **Provide autonomy:** Empower individuals and teams to make decisions and take ownership of their projects. This can help foster creativity and innovation by allowing individuals to explore and experiment without being overly constrained or micromanaged.
13. **Encourage continuous learning:** Encourage individuals and teams to continuously learn, both formally and informally. This can include attending conferences, taking courses, and engaging in self-directed learning.

14. **Foster a customer-centric mindset:** Encourage individuals and teams to adopt a customer-centric mindset, where the focus is on understanding and meeting the needs of the customer. This can help ensure that innovative ideas and solutions are developed with the customer in mind.
15. **Embrace emerging technologies:** Encourage individuals and teams to stay up to date with emerging technologies and trends. This can help identify new opportunities and enable the development of innovative solutions.

By following these tips, you can create a culture of innovation that encourages collaboration, experimentation, and creativity. This can help drive the development of products and solutions that meet the needs of your customers and position your organization for long-term success.

**Sales ethics and compliance** are essential components of any successful business that seeks to build and maintain a culture of integrity. Ethical sales practices ensure that customers are treated fairly and honestly, while compliance ensures that a company operates within the legal and regulatory framework governing its industry.

Here are some best practices for ethical sales and compliance:

1. **Develop a Code of Ethics:** Establish a code of ethics that outlines the principles and values that guide your sales team's behavior. This code should be communicated to all employees and integrated into your company's culture.
2. **Provide Training:** Provide regular training on ethical sales practices and compliance to ensure that your sales team understands the importance of ethical behavior and is equipped to comply with legal and regulatory requirements.
3. **Conduct Due Diligence:** Conduct due diligence on potential customers and partners to ensure that they are reputable and ethical. This can help prevent your company from being associated with unethical or illegal behavior.
4. **Avoid Conflicts of Interest:** Avoid conflicts of interest by disclosing any potential conflicts to customers and refrain from engaging in activities that could compromise your objectivity.
5. **Monitor Performance:** Regularly monitor your sales team's performance to ensure that they are adhering to ethical sales

practices and compliance requirements.

6. **Encourage Reporting:** Encourage employees to report any ethical violations or compliance concerns without fear of retaliation.
7. **Take Action:** Take swift and appropriate action when ethical violations or compliance issues arise. This demonstrates your commitment to ethical behavior and helps maintain your company's reputation.
8. **Foster a Culture of Accountability:** Create a culture of accountability to ensure that employees take responsibility for their actions. This includes holding employees accountable for ethical violations or compliance issues and rewarding employees who consistently exhibit ethical behavior.
9. **Provide Resources:** Provide your sales team with the resources they need to comply with legal and regulatory requirements. This may include access to legal counsel, compliance training, and other resources.
10. **Emphasize Customer Service:** Emphasize the importance of customer service in your sales process. This means prioritizing the needs and interests of your customers and striving to build long-term relationships based on trust and mutual benefit.
11. **Conduct Regular Audits:** Conduct regular audits to ensure that your sales team is complying with legal and regulatory requirements. This can help identify potential issues before they become major problems.
12. **Stay Up to Date:** Stay up to date on changes to laws and regulations that affect your industry and adjust your sales practices accordingly. This demonstrates your commitment

to compliance and helps ensure that your sales team is always operating within the bounds of the law.

13. **Encourage Feedback:** Encourage feedback from your customers and employees to identify areas for improvement in your sales processes. This can help you identify potential ethical or compliance issues and address them proactively.
14. **Implement a Whistleblower Policy:** Implement a whistleblower policy that allows employees to report ethical violations or compliance concerns anonymously and without fear of retaliation. This can help identify and address potential issues before they become major problems.
15. **Lead by Example:** Leaders should lead by example and model ethical behavior for their employees. This includes adhering to the company's code of ethics, complying with legal and regulatory requirements, and prioritizing customer service.
16. **Set Realistic Sales Targets:** Set realistic sales targets that are achievable without resorting to unethical or illegal behavior. This can help reduce the pressure on your sales team to engage in unethical or illegal behavior to meet unrealistic targets.
17. **Monitor Third-Party Vendors:** If you work with third-party vendors or suppliers, monitor their behavior to ensure that they are operating ethically and within the bounds of the law. This can help prevent your company from being associated with unethical or illegal behavior.
18. **Conduct Due Diligence on Sales Prospects:** Before engaging with a potential customer, conduct due diligence to ensure that they are a good fit for your company and that they operate ethically.

19. **Document Sales Processes:** Document your sales processes to ensure that they are transparent and can be audited if necessary. This can help identify potential issues and address them proactively.
20. **Conduct Regular Training:** Conduct regular training sessions to reinforce the importance of ethical behavior and compliance. This can help ensure that your sales team is always up to date on the latest best practices and legal and regulatory requirements.

By implementing these best practices, you can promote ethical sales and compliance within your organization, build trust with your customers, and maintain your reputation.

**Sales leadership and management** are indeed critical for ensuring the success of your sales team. Here are some best practices for effective sales leadership:

1. **Set clear expectations and goals:** As a sales leader, it is essential to set clear expectations and goals for your team. Ensure that everyone understands what is expected of them, and what they need to achieve. This will help to ensure that everyone is aligned and working towards a common goal.
2. **Provide regular feedback:** Regular feedback is essential for sales team members to understand how they are performing and where they need to improve. Provide feedback on both the positives and negatives and be specific about what needs to change.
3. **Provide training and coaching:** To help your sales team members reach their full potential, provide them with the necessary training and coaching. This will help to improve their skills and knowledge and make them more effective in their roles.
4. **Lead by example:** As a sales leader, it is essential to lead by example. Your team will take cues from you, and if you demonstrate a strong work ethic and commitment to success, they will likely follow suit.
5. **Foster a positive and collaborative team culture:** A positive and collaborative team culture is essential for sales success. Encourage teamwork, celebrate wins, and create a supportive environment where team members feel comfortable sharing ideas and feedback.

To develop your **skills as a sales manager**, consider the following:

1. **Continuously learn:** The sales landscape is constantly evolving, so it's important to keep learning and staying up to date with industry trends, best practices, and new technologies.
2. **Seek feedback:** Ask for feedback from your team members, peers, and superiors. This will help you identify areas where you can improve and make adjustments.
3. **Network:** Networking with other sales leaders and managers can be a great way to learn from others and stay connected to the broader industry.
4. **Be open to change:** Be open to new ideas and approaches and be willing to adapt your strategies as needed.
5. **Invest in yourself:** Consider attending sales training programs, reading sales books, or working with a sales coach to help you develop your skills and become a more effective sales leader.
6. **Understand your team:** Take the time to get to know your team members. Understand their strengths and weaknesses, as well as what motivates them. This will help you tailor your leadership style to each individual and create a more effective team.
7. **Communicate effectively:** Effective communication is crucial for sales leadership. Ensure that you are communicating clearly, listening actively, and providing feedback and guidance in a way that is constructive and

actionable.

8. **Embrace technology:** Technology can be a powerful tool for sales leadership. Consider leveraging tools such as CRM software, analytics platforms, and communication tools to help you manage your team more effectively.
9. **Focus on results:** Ultimately, the success of your sales team will be measured by their results. As a sales leader, it is essential to focus on achieving your sales targets and driving revenue growth.
10. **Build relationships:** Building strong relationships with your team members, customers, and stakeholders is essential for sales success. Prioritize relationship-building and invest in developing strong connections with those around you.
11. **Build a strong sales culture:** A strong sales culture is essential for driving success. This includes creating a sense of purpose, setting high standards, and fostering a competitive but collaborative environment.
12. **Lead with empathy:** Empathy is a critical skill for sales leadership. By understanding your team members' perspectives and experiences, you can build stronger relationships, foster trust, and create a more supportive work environment.
13. **Celebrate wins and learn from losses:** Celebrating wins and learning from losses is essential for building a successful sales team. Recognize and celebrate successes and use failures as opportunities for growth and improvement.
14. **Develop a strong hiring process:** Hiring the right people is essential for building a strong sales team. Develop a strong hiring process that focuses on identifying candidates with the right skills, experience, and cultural fit.

15. **Invest in your team's development:** Investing in your team's development is essential for driving long-term success. Provide ongoing training, coaching, and professional development opportunities to help your team members grow and thrive.

In a rapidly evolving sales landscape, effective sales leadership and management are essential for driving success. By focusing on the right skills, strategies, and practices, you can develop the skills you need to build a high-performing sales team and achieve your business goals.

**Business development and sales** are both critical components of a company's growth strategy, but they serve different purposes. Business development involves identifying new opportunities for growth, which may include expanding into new markets, developing new products or services, or forming strategic partnerships with other companies. Meanwhile, sales involve converting prospects into paying customers by persuading them to buy your products or services.

Integrating business development with your sales efforts can help you achieve your growth goals more effectively. Here are some best practices for doing so:

1. **Start with a clear strategy:** Before you can integrate business development and sales, you need to have a clear strategy for both. This should include specific goals and metrics for both teams, as well as a plan for how they will work together.
2. **Foster collaboration:** Encourage collaboration between your business development and sales teams. This can be done through regular meetings, joint training sessions, and shared communication channels.
3. **Use data to inform your approach:** Use data to identify potential new markets, target customers, and sales opportunities. This can help you refine your approach and ensure that you are targeting the right prospects.
4. **Prioritize relationship-building:** Business development is often about building relationships with potential partners or customers. Encourage your teams to prioritize relationship-

building efforts, such as attending industry events and conferences, networking with other professionals, and reaching out to potential partners or customers.

5. **Align incentives:** Align the incentives of your business development and sales teams to ensure that they are working towards the same goals. This may involve offering bonuses or other incentives for achieving specific targets or collaborating effectively.
6. **Leverage technology:** Use technology to streamline your business development and sales processes. This can include customer relationship management (CRM) tools to manage your sales pipeline, marketing automation tools to nurture leads, and data analytics tools to track your progress.
7. **Develop a strong value proposition:** Develop a strong value proposition that highlights the unique benefits of your product or service. This can help your sales team better communicate the value of your offering to potential customers.
8. **Focus on customer needs:** When developing new products or services, focus on meeting the needs of your target customers. This can help you develop offerings that are more likely to succeed in the market.
9. **Stay agile:** Stay agile and be willing to pivot your strategy if necessary. This may involve adjusting your target market, refining your value proposition, or pursuing new partnerships.
10. **Measure and optimize:** Measure the performance of your business development and sales efforts regularly and use this data to optimize your approach. This can help you identify areas for improvement and make data-driven decisions to

improve your results.

11. **Leverage social media:** Use social media to connect with potential customers, partners, and industry influencers. This can help you build your brand, expand your reach, and identify new opportunities for growth.
12. **Stay up to date on industry trends:** Stay up to date on industry trends and changes in the market. This can help you identify new opportunities for growth and adjust your strategy as needed.
13. **Build a strong company culture:** Build a strong company culture that supports collaboration, innovation, and growth. This can help you attract and retain top talent and create a more effective and cohesive team.
14. **Develop a strong brand:** Develop a strong brand that resonates with your target audience. This can help you differentiate yourself from competitors and build trust with potential customers.
15. **Invest in training and development:** Invest in training and development for your business development and sales teams. This can help them stay up to date on the latest best practices and industry trends and develop the skills they need to be successful in their roles.

Integrating business development with your sales efforts requires a holistic approach that involves many different factors. By leveraging technology, staying up to date on industry trends, and investing in your team, you can create a more effective and successful growth strategy for your company.

**Executing your sales strategy** effectively is crucial for the success of your business. Here are some best practices for executing your sales strategy and adapting it to changing market conditions:

1. **Define clear goals and objectives:** Before executing your sales strategy, you must have a clear understanding of your business goals and objectives. This will help you align your sales strategy with your overall business strategy and ensure that your sales efforts are focused on achieving specific outcomes.
2. **Identify your target market:** Knowing your target market is essential for developing an effective sales strategy. You need to understand your customers' needs, preferences, and behaviors to create a sales strategy that resonates with them.
3. **Develop a sales process:** A well-defined sales process is critical for executing your sales strategy effectively. It should include all the steps from lead generation to closing the deal and follow-up activities.
4. **Build a strong sales team:** Your sales team is the key to executing your sales strategy effectively. They should be knowledgeable about your products and services, have excellent communication and negotiation skills, and be passionate about selling.
5. **Monitor and measure performance:** Regularly monitoring and measuring your sales team's performance is essential for identifying areas for improvement and making necessary adjustments to your sales strategy.

6. **Adapt to changing market conditions:** The market is constantly changing, and your sales strategy should be flexible enough to adapt to these changes. Keep an eye on market trends, customer needs, and competitor activities, and adjust your sales strategy accordingly.
7. **Continuously improve your sales strategy:** Regularly review and analyze your sales strategy to identify areas for improvement. Solicit feedback from your sales team and customers to gain insights into what's working and what's not and use this information to refine your sales strategy.
8. **Leverage technology:** Technology can play a significant role in executing your sales strategy. Use tools such as customer relationship management (CRM) software, sales automation software, and data analytics to streamline your sales process, improve productivity, and gain insights into customer behavior.
9. **Focus on customer experience:** Providing an exceptional customer experience is critical for retaining customers and driving repeat business. Ensure that your sales strategy focuses on creating a positive customer experience from the initial contact through post-sale support.
10. **Stay agile:** In today's fast-paced business environment, agility is essential. Your sales strategy should be flexible enough to respond quickly to changing market conditions, customer needs, and emerging trends.
11. **Foster collaboration:** Collaboration between sales and other departments such as marketing, customer service, and product development can help to align your sales strategy with your overall business strategy. Encourage collaboration and communication between departments to ensure that

your sales efforts are integrated with other areas of your business.

12. **Invest in training and development:** Providing ongoing training and development opportunities for your sales team is critical for executing your sales strategy effectively. Ensure that your sales team has the knowledge, skills, and resources they need to succeed.
13. **Monitor your competition:** Keep a close eye on your competitors' activities and adjust your sales strategy accordingly. Analyze their strengths and weaknesses and use this information to differentiate your products or services and gain a competitive advantage.

In conclusion, executing your sales strategy effectively requires a combination of best practices, including a clear understanding of your business goals, a well-defined sales process, a strong sales team, a willingness to adapt to changing market conditions, and the use of technology. By following these tips, you can create a sales strategy that drives business growth and success.

# AUTHORS NOTE

As a leadership mentor, I am dedicated to helping individuals achieve their full potential by providing guidance, support, and practical tools for effective leadership. With a proven track record of success, I bring a unique combination of expertise in leadership development, strategy, and communication to every individual engagement.

My approach to leadership mentoring is characterized by a deep commitment to understanding each individual's unique strengths, challenges, and goals. I work closely with individuals to identify their areas of growth and develop personalized strategies for achieving success. I help individuals build the skills, knowledge, and confidence they need to lead effectively in any situation.

Whether working with emerging leaders or seasoned executives, I am known for my ability to foster meaningful connections and create a safe and supportive learning environment. By leveraging my extensive experience in leadership development, I help individuals navigate complex challenges, overcome obstacles, and achieve their goals with confidence and clarity.

Throughout my career as a leadership mentor, I have helped individuals and organizations achieve significant breakthroughs in their leadership development. I am committed to staying at the forefront of the latest trends and best practices in leadership, and I regularly engage in ongoing professional development to ensure that individuals receive the highest quality guidance and support. Ultimately, my goal as a leadership mentor is to help individuals become the best leaders they can be, so they can make a positive impact in their organizations and communities.

# ABOUT THE AUTHOR

Digvijay Mourya, a highly accomplished chemical engineer with an MBA, has over 35 years of work experience, including 20 years in leadership positions. He has contributed significantly to the field of chemical engineering and has demonstrated exceptional leadership skills throughout his career.

Currently, Digvijay Mourya serves as the CEO of an industrial house and oversees all operations and strategic initiatives. Under his leadership, the company has achieved significant growth and success, expanding its reach to new markets, and driving innovation in the industry.

Before his current role, Digvijay Mourya held various leadership positions in several renowned organizations, where he was responsible for developing and executing business strategies, managing teams, and driving growth.

Beyond his professional achievements, Digvijay Mourya is known for his integrity, dedication, and passion for mentoring young professionals. He is committed to giving back to his community and has been actively involved in several social and environmental initiatives.

Overall, Digvijay Mourya's extensive work experience, exceptional leadership skills, and commitment to excellence make him a highly respected and sought-after professional in the industry.

www.ingramcontent.com/pod-product-compliance
Lightning Source LLC
LaVergne TN
LVHW012058160826
845678LV00014B/2869

* 9 7 8 8 1 9 6 0 8 9 5 2 8 *